Green Reflections

The Bible Reading Fellowship
15 The Chambers, Vineyard
Abingdon OX14 3FE
brf.org.uk

The Bible Reading Fellowship (BRF) is a Registered Charity (233280)

ISBN 978 1 80039 068 3
First published 2021
10 9 8 7 6 5 4 3 2 1 0
All rights reserved

A catalogue record for this book is available from the British Library

Printed and bound in the UK by Zenith Media

Green Reflections

Biblical inspiration for sustainable living

Martin J. Hodson and Margot R. Hodson

Paintings by Martin Beek

This book is dedicated to our friends in **Sage, Oxford's Christian environmental group**. Thank you for travelling with us over the 30 years of Sage and we remember with thanks those whose journey in this life has ended. We will meet again in the new creation!

We are very grateful to Olivia Warburton, Daniele Och and the staff at The Bible Reading Fellowship for their patience and advice during the publication process.

Thanks to Lisa Cherrett, Eley McAinsh and Andrew Roberts for inviting us to write for them, and then skilfully editing our various reflections. Martin Beek's artwork is superb, and we are immensely grateful that it could be used in our book.

Contents

 # Introduction

Welcome to *Green Reflections*. We hope that you will find this book a useful resource. We love writing biblical reflections and are grateful to The Bible Reading Fellowship for giving us several opportunities to do this. Our particular interest is in the environment, and so our reflections have always had a green flavour. With the publication of the second edition of *A Christian Guide to Environmental Issues* (BRF, 2021) we wanted a more reflective resource to go with it.

The idea came to bring together all of the reflections that we had written for BRF over the past few years under one roof. The reflections Margot wrote for *Guidelines* in 2013 have been updated, and they provide a biblical introduction to creation care. We have also written three sets of reflections for *Bible Reflections for Older People*, starting with 'The wisdom of trees'. The focus of these reflections is more pastoral and spiritual. We soon discovered that you don't need to be an older person to use these and like them!

Our most practical set of reflections were written for *Holy Habits Bible Reflections: Sharing Resources*. Not all of these are obviously 'green', but we would argue that the whole idea of sharing resources is environmentally friendly.

The final set we wrote specially to accompany the second edition of *A Christian Guide to Environmental Issues* and look at all the issues covered in that book, including climate change and biodiversity loss. They end with a focus on hope.

In total we have 62 reflections. Amazingly, after all this reflection writing, we only have one passage that was used twice! We have arranged them so that the more pastoral and spiritual reflections interweave with the others. This is so that a person using the reflections daily and sequentially will have a more varied diet than if we had blocked all the pastoral and spiritual reflections together.

How can you use these reflections? The obvious way would be to read one reflection a day as part of your daily devotions. If you did that you would have enough for two months. But there are other ways of using this resource.

You might be running a day at your church looking at climate change, and want a few biblical reflections to intersperse with the science, theology and practical responses. Look up 'climate change' in the index of themes, and see if any of the reflections referenced matches your needs.

You might have to write a sermon or lead a Bible study on a passage or topic. Again, look at the indexes in the back of the book. You might use some of these reflections in conjunction with the Bible studies at the end of each chapter in *A Christian Guide to Environmental Issues*.

Then you might get really inventive. We were once invited to a retreat day where the leader had taken our reflections on 'The wisdom of trees' and found all sorts of foods and items to represent the different tree species. Then we ate or looked at each of these as the reflections were read out to the assembled group. Let us know if you do something like that!

There now follow brief descriptions of the six series of reflections. Our prayer is that however you use them, these reflections will inspire you to take better care of God's wonderful creation.

1   The wisdom of trees

Trees are mentioned hundreds of times in the Bible and were used to teach spiritual truths. These reflections use the trees as our teachers. By understanding some of the spiritual truths important for the Bible's first hearers, we find out how they apply to our lives today.

2   Biblical guidelines for understanding the environment

These studies explore the biblical basis for valuing and caring for creation. Covering both Old and New Testament readings, we discover how the Bible can help us understand God's love for his creation and our role in caring for it as part of Christian discipleship and mission.

3   Landscapes of promise

Our journey through life takes us through many different landscapes, and we can learn about ourselves when the geography around us changes. These reflections take different biblical landscapes, and we learn how God can speak to us at all stages of our life's journey.

4 Sharing resources

The book of Acts presents a way of Christian living where all things were shared widely. These studies dig into some Old Testament passages exploring the biblical teaching on sharing: how to live compassionately in a world of limited resources, as we draw from the generous and persistent giving of God.

5 Storms and fair weather

The Bible is full of weather. Through different weather, God's people learned how to depend on him and how to follow him in all circumstances. We hope these studies guide you to see the brightening hand of God working in your life, through storms and fair weather, to lead you to know him better.

6 Christian reflections on environmental issues

These studies are a companion to *A Christian Guide to Environmental Issues*. With an introduction on love and a conclusion on hope, they take eight contemporary environmental issues and reflect on them from a biblical perspective.

1

The wisdom of trees

Do you have memories of particular trees? We can each remember climbing trees as children; as adults, we had an apple tree that was especially fruitful at our last house, and now we have a beautiful lime tree. Trees can act as markers through our lives. Often in the background but always giving context, pointing back to the past and forward to the future.

Trees are mentioned hundreds of times in the Bible and in almost every book. Many of these are geographical, helping to show where a story is set, but sometimes trees are used to teach spiritual truths.

These reflections will use the trees as our teachers. We will begin to learn some of the spiritual truths that the Bible's first hearers would have understood, and find out how they apply to our lives today. We will discover how we can be sustained by our roots like the willow and bear fruit like the palm tree even when we stay still and the world changes around us.

So please join us on a spiritual journey through the Bible's woodland and find some truths for your own life from these majestic teachers.

First published in *Bible Reflections for Older People*, September–December 2018.

1 Mustard-seed faith

Matthew 17:20

[Jesus] replied, 'Because you have so little faith. Truly I tell you, if you have faith as small as a mustard seed, you can say to this mountain, "Move from here to there," and it will move. Nothing will be impossible for you.'

The mustard seed appears in two stories in the gospels, one concerning the kingdom of heaven (Matthew 13:31–32) and the other, faith. Botanists have debated which plant species Jesus is referring to in these accounts, as the mustard seed is not that small and its plant is at best a fair-sized shrub (certainly not a tree). But let's put aside the arguments over species and think more generally about seeds and trees. We did a rough calculation and reckon that a mature oak tree is about three million times the weight of an acorn.

The good news is that Jesus clearly tells us that we don't need faith the size of a massive tree, only a small seed's worth. Just a small amount of faith can move mountains. What is it that you need faith for in your life at the moment? It may be a health issue, an upcoming house move or perhaps something you need to talk to a friend about. Remember the mustard seed and have faith.

PRAYER
Lord,
we know that sometimes our faith can seem very small.
Show us how to use that small amount of faith
to build your kingdom.
Amen

2 Peace of the olive

Genesis 8:11a

When the dove returned to [Noah] in the evening, there in its beak was a freshly plucked olive leaf!

At home, we have an olive-wood holding cross, which is smooth and curved and sits easily in the palm of a hand. It is a reminder of the transforming power of Christ and the connection between his suffering, redemption and healing. The olive is a long-lived tree and highly prized for its fruit. Olive oil is liquid gold, as it provides food, light and heat. Priests and kings were anointed with olive oil as they entered service and Jesus' disciples used the oil for healing (Mark 6:13).

The olive tree is first mentioned in the Bible at the end of the flood. Noah sends out a dove and he returns with a sprig of olive, proving the existence of dry land. Because of this story, the olive is a symbol of peace-making and reconciliation. It was no coincidence that Jesus prayed in an olive grove, Gethsemane, as he awaited arrest on his journey to the cross.

Peace can seem an elusive dream for communities and families who long for harmony. The olive reminds us that there is hope. Jesus died and rose again so that one day all things will be reconciled (Colossians 1:20). We can trust Christ's reconciling power working in our world and in our own lives, families and communities.

PRAYER
Heavenly Father,
help us to be bearers of olive branches
and bringers of peace.
Amen

3 Oaks of righteousness

Isaiah 61:3b

They will be called oaks of righteousness, a planting of the Lord for the display of his splendour.

There is some confusion over the word 'oak' in the Bible. If you look at different translations, sometimes the word 'terebinth' (the tree which produces the pistachio nut) is used and sometimes they cannot decide what species it is and just use the word 'tree'. Whatever the case, these trees were often planted at places of worship, and sometimes they were places where loved ones were buried. They symbolised strength, wisdom, longevity and, here, righteousness.

Are we oaks of righteousness? Whatever stage of life we are at, we should all be aiming to live righteous lives. We have been planted where we find ourselves at this time to 'display his splendour'. So we are not living lives that are honouring to God just for ourselves, but because we are God's witnesses to this world. It is not always easy to decide what is the right action to take, but we should definitely avoid things that we know to be wrong. And God will help us with both of these. We just need to ask for his help in prayer.

PRAYER
Lord,
we pray for people who have been given positions of responsibility.
They might be church ministers, leaders of businesses or politicians.
We pray that they will lead us in paths of righteousness.
Amen

4 See the almond tree

Jeremiah 1:11–12

The word of the Lord came to me: 'What do you see, Jeremiah?' 'I see the branch of an almond tree,' I replied. The Lord said to me, 'You have seen correctly, for I am watching to see that my word is fulfilled.'

The almond is a beautiful tree. It is the first to flower each year, and its Hebrew name means 'hard-working', 'reliable' and 'watching'. Its lovely blossom certainly seems to watch over the Mediterranean landscape as it signals the start of spring.

As the seasons shift in our lives, we can find ourselves to be like almond trees. We are looked to for wisdom and reliability at work, in church and with our families, as younger generations face multiple challenges. Even when retired, there are plenty of opportunities for hard work, with family and community. We also find ourselves watching. There are many good things to look out for, such as children succeeding in college and careers, a first grandchild or even a great-grandchild. There are also difficult things to see: illness and bereavement, marriage breakdown, redundancy or ageing church communities.

God promised Jeremiah that he was watching. When we feel powerless, he is along-side, working in the lives of the people we love and the situations that we care about. He will see his word fulfilled, and one day we will see it blossom like an almond tree.

PRAYER
Dear Lord,
give us strength to be prayerful watchers
and give us wisdom to support those we love.
Amen

5 Cedar of Lebanon

Judges 9:15

The thornbush said to the trees, 'If you really want to anoint me king over you, come and take refuge in my shade; but if not, then let fire come out of the thornbush and consume the cedars of Lebanon!'

Cedars of Lebanon are majestic, long-lived trees native to Lebanon. They appear numerous times in the Bible, but only in the Old Testament. Many times, they are mentioned as being used to build Solomon's temple. Their wood was highly prized, as it was strong, aromatic and resistant to attack by insects and decay.

This story in Judges 9 repays reading in full. Abimelek becomes king by killing the 70 sons of Jerub-Baal. Jotham, the youngest son, escapes, and tells a parable to the people of Shechem and Beth Millo in which the trees are all offered the chance to be king over the other trees. One by one, they refuse. Finally, the thorn-bush is made the offer. He sees the cedar of Lebanon as the true king of the trees but threatens that fire could come out of him to consume the much larger tree.

The cedar is the king of the trees, but who is king of your heart? Jesus, like the cedar, is strong, a majestic king and someone you can rely on.

PRAYER
Lord Jesus,
we pray that you will rule over us,
and we ask for your strength wherever we are now.
Amen

6 Willow roots

Jeremiah 17:7–8a

But blessed is the one who trusts in the Lord, whose confidence is in him. They will be like a tree planted by the water that sends out its roots by the stream.

For many years, we taught at a summer school near Berlin for young Christian adults. We stayed by a lake, and there was a large willow tree right by the water. The willow had its roots deep down into the fertile and well-watered soil of the lakeside. Our students were likewise putting down roots into the Christian faith that would hopefully last a lifetime.

If you have had the privilege of becoming a Christian as a young person and have kept an active faith, you will have those deep roots to draw on as you meet new challenges in later life. If you are still relatively new to faith or exploring faith, the good news is that it is never too late to put down roots.

With roots deep in the riverside soil, our willow need not fear, even in a heat wave. It can be devastating when health breaks down or we are shattered by bereavement, but if we nurture our roots, such as through the habit of daily Bible reading, we can find comfort and peace in the same slow, steady way that roots supply water for the tree.

PRAYER
Lord,
help me to put down roots of faith
and to trust you in all the seasons of life.
Amen

7 To plant a tamarisk

Genesis 21:33 (NRSV)

Abraham planted a tamarisk tree in Beersheba, and called there on the name of the Lord, the Everlasting God.

Tamarisks are shrubby trees that can reach ten metres in height. They grow mostly in deserts and wadis, and are very tolerant of drought and salinity. The Bedouin often plant them for shade.

Why did Abraham plant a tamarisk tree at Beersheba? Nobody knows for sure, but if you read earlier in chapter 21 it gives some clues. Beersheba means 'well of seven' or 'well of the oath'. Abraham came to an agreement with Abimelek over a well, and they swore an oath to each other at this spot. It was this that allowed Abraham and his family to remain in Canaan, so it was a very important event. Trees were seen as symbols of life and of blessing by God. On other occasions, Abraham built an altar to honour God, but here it seems he planted a tree.

How do we honour God? We may not build altars or plant trees, but we should all be honouring God in some way. We will honour God by the kind of life that we lead. Whatever our age and whatever our circumstances, we should aim to live lives that will please God.

PRAYER
Lord Jesus,
show me how I can live a better life and one that is pleasing to you.
Show me how to be a good witness to the Everlasting God.
Amen

8 The fruitful palm

Psalm 92:12–15 (abridged)

The righteous will flourish like a palm tree... planted in the house of the Lord... They will still bear fruit in old age, they will stay fresh and green, proclaiming, 'The Lord is upright; he is my Rock.'

In the Old City of Jerusalem stands Christ Church, the oldest Anglican church in the Middle East. In the garden grows a palm tree. Its age and fruitfulness point to the fruitful ministry of the church.

Date palms have been cultivated for at least 9,000 years. They probably originated in what is now Iraq and were a familiar fruit throughout the Bible. In Israel, their branches are cut for the autumn Feast of Tabernacles. Jesus entered Jerusalem to the waving of palm branches. The strong and steady palm tree at Christ Church could tell many stories from the drama of history, yet it still bears fruit.

We each have a story to tell and have each seen many changes that have happened around us. In this life, we will never fully know the fruit of our own lives. Every one of us can look back with thanks for something in our past, and we still have opportunities to bear fruit today. For some that might be in an active way; for others it might be in stillness and prayer, remembering those who care for us and those we love.

PRAYER
Dear Lord,
remind us of things we can give thanks for in our lives
yesterday and today.
Amen

9 Love the pomegranate

Song of Solomon 4:3

Your lips are like a scarlet ribbon; your mouth is lovely. Your temples behind your veil are like the halves of a pomegranate.

Pomegranates are common in Israel and are frequently cultivated. The plant is a small shrub, the flowers are red and the fruit is round and multicoloured: pink, yellow and purple. Each fruit has many seeds; the rabbis reckon there are 613, one for each of the commandments of the law. Pomegranates often symbolise fruitfulness and fertility.

Ornamental pomegranates were used on some of the priestly garments and were engraved as decorations in the temple in Jerusalem. They are also found in the love poem the Song of Solomon (or Song of Songs). In chapter 4, a man describes a woman in a glowing and poetic way. The word 'temples' could also be translated 'cheeks'. The book is often taken to be an allegory for the love of God for his people.

As we grow older, love takes on a different meaning. We may not be quite as passionate as we once were (but we might be!). We may have lost a loved one some years ago, but still love them with all our heart. Love between people changes over time. But one thing never, ever changes and that is the love of God.

PRAYER
Lord God,
we thank you for loving us
even when we are far from perfect.
Show us how to love you more.
Amen

10 Tree of life

Revelation 22:2b

On each side of the river stood the tree of life, bearing twelve crops of fruit, yielding its fruit every month. And the leaves of the tree are for the healing of the nations.

The most famous tree in the Bible is the tree of life. We find it in Genesis 3:24, where God protects it from humans after the fall, because its fruit gives eternal life. It appears in Proverbs 3:18, where it is linked to wisdom. Then, it is finally found in Revelation as trees on either side of the river of life, coming out of the new Jerusalem. It bears a different fruit each month and its leaves are 'for the healing of the nations'.

When we are young, we may believe that our generation can change the world to be a more peaceful, equitable place. When we look at the global tensions as older people, we realise that no generation has been able to end war and bring healing. Jesus promises that, one day, he will return to bring in the new creation, where conflict will be no more.

Meanwhile, we can pray for healing and, as Christ's body, for the church to be those healing leaves to those around us. We find this is no utopia but a practical way of living that makes the future real in the present.

PRAYER
Heavenly Father,
help us to look to your new creation
and to point towards it in all that we do.
Amen

2

Biblical guidelines for understanding the environment

On New Year's Day 2020, we went for a beautiful walk in the west Oxfordshire countryside with our old friends from Sage, Oxford's Christian environmental group. It was a fantastic day and the local countryside was glorious. There is a timelessness about nature and, looking around, we could be forgiven for thinking that all is well with the earth.

But the environment continues to be in our news and, sadly, the reports are not good ones. At that time wildfires were raging through Australia, and this was to be repeated later in the year in California, Oregon and Washington State. It became apparent that 2020 was also a year of extreme activity for hurricanes and tropical storms in the Atlantic. Several caused major damage. There have been disturbing reports from the Arctic and Antarctic concerning the melting of their icecaps. We know that 2020 tied with 2016 as the warmest on record.

These are weather impacts that we would expect to see if our climate were warming up, and the impacts are felt most strongly in some of the poorest parts of the world. Climate change is not the only environmental problem that we face this century. In 2020, global human population reached 7.8 billion – over four times what it was

100 years ago. We are seeing a huge decline in biodiversity, with WWF reporting that we have seen a 68 per cent decline in monitored vertebrate species populations between 1970 and 2016. Water scarcity is becoming an issue worldwide.

What we did not know when we walked on 1 January 2020 was that the Covid-19 pandemic was brewing in Wuhan, China, a place that few of us had heard of before. The evidence strongly suggests that this pandemic, like those before it, was caused primarily by our terrible treatment of the environment.

So the natural world is in a sorry state. How do we understand this as Christians, and how should we respond?

In the next twelve reflections we are going to explore a biblical basis for valuing and caring for creation. In the first six we will consider the Old Testament; the second six will focus on the New Testament and our relationship with nature from a gospel perspective. Overall, we will see how the Bible provides a fresh approach to tackling a number of contemporary problems. We will also look at some practical issues in our own lives, and finally we shall explore the Christian message of hope. This is vital for us and also for many people in the wider community who have lost confidence in the future.

The Hebrew scriptures have much to teach us about the natural world, and it is perhaps not surprising that there are more Old Testament readings used in this book than those from the New Testament. We should remember that for the writers of the New Testament, their Bible was the Old Testament. They did not need to go over that material again. Moreover, apart from the gospels, the New Testament writers were writing in an urban context. Nevertheless, the New Testament does have vital teaching about the connection between creation and redemption. It particularly shows us where Jesus fits into environmental theology and develops this teaching through key themes, such as incarnation, resurrection and salvation.

In all these passages, there is a sense of dependence on the relationships between God, people and planet. When humanity is reconciled with God, harmony in the other relationships follows. When humanity walks away from God, we find that human relationships are fraught and nature suffers. The overall theme is of a beautiful creation made by God, which has been damaged through careless treatment by humans.

We might think that the ideal future would be a return to the wild, living in amazing forests and mountain ranges. Although these environments are portrayed as precious to God, the future place shown for humans to inhabit is one that has been formed in interaction with humans. We are called to get involved with God's creation. Looking at our world today, this is a call not only to farm the land but also to take positive action to reduce climate change and restore the places that others have devastated.

This set of reflections use longer Bible passages, and you will need to read these in your own Bible before looking at the reflections.

First published in *Guidelines*, January–April 2013; updated in 2020.

1 A good creation

Genesis 1:1–25

The opening words of Genesis are majestic. The writer declares that God is before everything and that he created everything. Whatever the mechanism of creation, Genesis declares that it has its origins in a creator God.

The word 'good' is used seven times in this chapter (seven being a symbol of perfection). God's creation is good – every bit of it. At different times in history, there have been debates over the goodness of the world. Some of the ancient Greek philosophers took a more negative view. Plato and some of his later followers, such as Plotinus, considered that goodness was only to be found in the higher spiritual realm. At different times in history, this thinking has led to a devaluing of our natural world, and, sadly, many Christians have absorbed it, wrongly believing it to be biblical Christian doctrine.

Yet the biblical text challenges this view. The material world is made by God, and he saw it as good before humans were created. The value God places on each part of creation is shown by the careful way in which the different aspects of the cosmos and our own planet are described. Each part of creation therefore has value in its own right, and we should approach it with the view that it belongs to God and not ourselves.

Sometimes, when people want to put forward reasons for looking after the environment better, they suggest human reasons for doing so. For example, they will say that there may be is a cure for cancer in the biodiversity of a tropical rainforest. Although this is very important, we also need to value nature for its own sake, because our creator God declared creation to be good before humans existed. The goodness of creation therefore depends on the value placed on it by God and not its usefulness to humans.

Our universe is finely tuned for life, and our planet has just the right conditions for life. Atheists sometimes use the 'multiverse' theory to explain this: they suggest that there are an infinite number of universes and that we happen to live on the one where everything is finely and exactly set up to support life. Faith in God seems more straightforward!

2 Humans and nature

Genesis 1:26–30

As Genesis 1 draws to a close, we see the creation of humans as the last stage of God's good creation. Here the attention turns to people – our food and our relationship with the rest of nature. Humans are commanded to be fruitful and fill the earth (v. 28). Does this sanction unlimited growth, or have we already fulfilled this commandment? Today our global food production depends heavily on nitrogen fertilisers, which are produced through the burning of fossil fuels with consequent carbon emissions. Much food goes to waste in the west, and land is not in full production. In poorer countries, the problems are often those of distribution and disruption through conflict. If we are to have a level of human population that can be sustained in the long term, we need to consider all these issues thoughtfully.

The command to 'subdue' the earth (v. 28) has been highlighted by those seeking to challenge the positive concept of biblical stewardship. The Hebrew word (*kabash*) literally means to 'tread down', but it is usually used to describe ploughing. Placed together with a command to reproduce, it provides a picture of humans farming the land to produce food for a growing family. We need to place this teaching alongside our study of Genesis 1:1–25. There should be a balance between adapting ecosystems for our own use and safeguarding nature because we recognise that it has value in its own right. How we can manage the balance of that relationship is explained as the biblical teaching on the environment unfolds.

The Hebrew word for 'rule' (*radah*) is a key concept in verse 28, but it is also controversial. The NRSV follows the King James Bible, translating it as 'dominion', which might imply an exploitative rule over the natural world. However, we detect a different meaning once we know that the same word is used to describe Solomon's God-given rule over Israel (1 Kings 4:24). To 'rule', in biblical thinking, means to be given a responsibility. The rule of humankind should be life-giving rather than exploitative. Jesus demonstrates this in his ministry – for example, in Matthew 8, where he heals several people and calms a storm on the Sea of Galilee. In these miracles, he demonstrates his lordship over creation.

Humanity has been given leadership over the rest of creation, as our very first responsibility. How well have we exercised it?

3 Rest and relationship

Genesis 2:1–15

Creation was not finished until the seventh day, when God created rest. Our beautiful world is full of complex cycles and changes of season, but rest is essential. God blessed this day of rest and made it holy. As we look at a succession of financial crises worldwide, we might reflect that a major reason why our world has slid into chaos is because we have ignored rest. Humanity has continued to use up resources without any thought of giving time to replenish stocks. Our economic system is based on the concept of continual growth, and yet our planet is finite. When we rest, our minds and bodies are restored and renewed. Rest periods are characteristic of all life on earth. Rest gives us the time to reflect on the other parts of our life. It is also a statement that we are content to have enough and not to work endlessly for more. We have worked our planet without rest, and the ecological crisis is a predictable result.

The text changes tone from verse 4, where we have a second account of creation, this time written in narrative form. We miss some of the nuance of this text in English translation. God forms human (*Adam*) out of the dust (*Adomah*). Literally,

God creates us from earth and calls us 'earthy'. This implies a deep connection between humans and our earth. We are a part of this creation and not separate from it. We need to regain this truth in order to make good decisions about how we provide leadership for the biodiversity of the earth.

God then created a beautiful garden for humans to live in. He placed them in the garden 'to work it and take care of it' (v. 15). These words are also important as we build a foundation for biblical creation care. The word 'work' (*avodah*) also means 'serve', and is used elsewhere to describe discipleship: we are called to love God and serve him with all our hearts and souls (Deuteronomy 10:12). The word translated 'take care of' is often translated as 'keep' (*shamah*) and is also found in the Aaronic blessing, 'The Lord bless you and keep you' (Numbers 6:24). In caring for the garden, we serve before the Lord and are called to care for it and protect it in the way that God cares for us. What a calling!

4 Called to the land and called to justice

Leviticus 25

In the opening sentences of Leviticus 25, there are two clear statements about human relationship with the land. First, the land is a gift of God: it belongs to him, not us. Second, we are called to respect limits and to have our sabbath rests, not simply each week but every one in seven years. In all of this we are called to be a part of a three-way relationship between God, people and planet.

Interestingly, this relationship with the land is not about a respect for nature pointing back to a hunter-gatherer existence. It is clear from this passage and those that we read earlier, in Genesis, that farming is the way in which we are expected to interact with the natural world in our daily lives. We are called to roll our sleeves up and get involved. Biblically, it is okay to make adaptations of natural systems and to live off the fruits of creation, but it is not okay to farm beyond the limits of the land. We must leave the edges of our fields for the poor (Leviticus 19:9–10). The land must have its year of rest, when, presumably, wildlife will also take their share of its bounty (25:7).

If these guidelines are kept, there is a promise that the people will live in safety and have food to eat (v. 19). Clearly that is not the case for the people of Kerala in India who have been affected by severe flooding in 2018, 2019 and 2020. Our collective loss of a sense of limit has led to our changing climate and many other environmental problems. Those suffering the consequences are often not those who have benefited from human overuse of the land.

Leviticus 25 provides a basis for a specific relationship to a specific land. Each tribe and family in Israel was given land as a gift from God, for themselves and for their descendants. If they fell into poverty and were forced to sell their land, their family could regain it in the year of jubilee. Today, many of the world's people live in cities, with global networks. We have lost the sense of connection to a specific location. We also need to regain our sense of relationship with our own land – be that rural or urban.

In both situations, God gives us land as a gift, and nature as a blessing. He asks that we care for the land in which he places us, including the human elements, such as buildings, as well as the natural environment. Urban areas can seem less connected with nature, and yet it is often the natural elements, such as trees and lawns, that make them attractive.

5 Going beyond limits

Genesis 3:1–19

The Amazon has the largest tropical rainforest in the world, and it is estimated that 10 per cent of the known species on earth reside there. Sadly already 20 per cent of the forest has been lost and more is being lost every year. There are many factors responsible for deforestation in the Amazon, including logging for timber, conversion of forest to agricultural land for growing soybeans and oil palm plantations, and cattle ranching.

Frequently the forest is burned in the process. In February 2020 it was reported that as much as one fifth of the Amazon rainforest was emitting more carbon than it was absorbing. The Amazon is often known as the 'lungs of the world'. It absorbs huge amounts of carbon dioxide and influences the global hydrological cycle and weather patterns. Worryingly it appears that global climate change is also causing severe droughts in parts of the Amazon. There have been three 'hundred year' droughts in 2005, 2010 and 2015. These led to the death of many trees and to even more carbon emissions. All of these factors make the future of the Amazon a major worry.

When we read the Genesis account of the fall of humanity, we usually see the taking of the forbidden fruit as an act of disobedience against God. It was disobedience that led to the expulsion from Eden. However, it is also significant to note that Eden's sin was greed.

Taking the forbidden fruit of Eden can be seen as a paradigm for the despoliation of the Amazon and Asian tropical forests. It parallels our disregard for the fragile ecology above the Alaskan oil reserves and our use of the earth's resources beyond its ability to regenerate. When will we learn the lesson of Eden? Possibly only when we experience the full consequences of our actions.

We should instead heed the practical words of Deuteronomy 20:19: 'When you lay siege to a city for a long time, fighting against it to capture it, do not destroy its trees by putting an axe to them, because you can eat their fruit. Do not cut them down. Are the trees of the field people, that you should besiege them?' This does not mean that it is acceptable for humans to go to war, but it does mean that nature should not be made the victim of human conflicts. We need to manage the resources of the planet for the good of all creatures.

6 The earth mourns

Hosea 4:1–3

Climate scientists predict an increase in floods and other extreme weather events as the planet warms through human-induced climate change. Jane Fucella is a friend of Margot's who worked with Interserve in Bangkok. In 2011 she wrote about the floods they had been experiencing:

> One third of the country is under water. Eight million people are directly affected. Well over 500 are dead – either drowned, electrocuted, bitten by snakes or dead through disease from floodwaters. Evacuation centres are full of people because the flood water is chest deep in their communities and houses. The water is black. Hundreds of crocodiles have escaped from farms and are on the loose. Those people who are still in their homes have no access to essential food and water. Sanitation is a disaster in flooded areas.

The words of Hosea seem strangely contemporary when read against such an account of devastation. Hosea saw a breakdown in the relationship between humans and God, which led to a breakdown in relationships among people and between humans and the rest of creation. Human injustice was rife and the inevitable result was bloodshed and pain.

An interesting phrase is found in verse 3: what does the writer mean by 'the land mourns'? The second half of the verse refers to the death of birds and fish. The biodiversity of the planet is adversely affected by our human conflicts and our consumerist greed. Once the relationships have broken down, human actions have no limitations and death and destruction are the inevitable consequences. This echoes the world described in Genesis 3, where we see that the land does not simply mourn but is cursed (3:17).

There are different views on the nature of the fall. Many scholars see it in terms of relationship breakdown. Others go further and support the idea of a cosmic fall. In the latter view, nature has been fundamentally damaged, even though fallen creation continues to bear God's image and fallen humanity continues to radiate God's goodness and creativity. (We will explain this thinking further in Reflection 9 on Romans 8:18–25, on page 52).

7 Born into his own creation

John 1:1–14

Most Christians will have particular memories of hearing this famous passage read. For many of us, it takes our thoughts to Christmas, when the focus is on the amazing truth that Jesus, the light of the world, was born among us – that God became human for our sake. So what has it got to do with ecology? The environmental focus of this passage comes from an understanding of how the doctrines of creation and incarnation interact.

Jesus is revealed here in three unique ways: existing before the world began, being divine and being the agent of creation. The passage reaches a climax in verse 14: 'the Word became flesh and made his dwelling among us'. The environmental implication of this statement is profound. When our holy and perfect Creator became a physical person, he affirmed the continuing goodness of his creation. In creating the universe, God brought light to the whole world. The darkness described in verse 5 is not part of God's good creation but is the very absence of that goodness. It is this darkness that has blinded human eyes, preventing people from recognising the light of Christ. Has it also led to their actions that have caused damage and destruction?

The logical conclusion is that when humanity embraces the light, it should also regain the Creator's love and care for his world. But what if the light has come purely to save humanity? This passage highlights the fact that humans can find full adoption as children of God through believing in Christ (vv. 12–13) and this gift is not offered to the rest of creation – but light is given to all. When God makes his dwelling among us, his glory shines through all creation. This idea picks up on a verse from Habakkuk: 'For the earth will be filled with the knowledge of the glory of the Lord as the waters cover the sea' (2:14).

8 The miraculous catch of fish

John 21:1–14

During the 20th century, two world wars provided unintentional 'sabbath rests' for global fish populations. Today, fish such as cod and haddock are being fished beyond their capacity to replenish. If we keep fishing at unsustainable levels, we will eventually drive some species to extinction.

The story of the miraculous catch of fish is a glimpse of the abundance of restored creation through the resurrection of Christ. Like the birth of Christ, his bodily resurrection affirms God's creation and God's continuing purpose for it. If creation was simply a backdrop and God wished to redeem humans alone into a 'higher' spiritual realm, we would expect Jesus to have been resurrected into a 'higher' non-physical form. This view might be attractive to those basing their views on Platonic thinking. In reality, though, Jesus rose in a new creation body that was physical: he could eat bread and fish; his disciples could touch him. The new creation we glimpse in the risen Christ is a real physical realm that is wonderfully perfected and free from sin and death.

The miraculous catch of fish is a window on this new creation. In our world, we will always struggle. Harvests will fail us, both on land and in the sea, as a result of natural problems and because of our own overuse of the planet. On that post-resurrection morning in Galilee, Jesus revealed the abundance of a restored creation to his disciples with a catch that was beyond the resources of our present world.

At breakfast, Jesus blessed and broke bread for his disciples. Each time we break bread at Communion, we are reminded of the abundant life and hope found in the new creation. When we eat bread in our daily lives, we are also reminded that Christ makes ordinary things extraordinary. In Christ, physical and spiritual are intertwined in this world and the next.

Thinking back to our world's fish stocks, we must examine our management of them. Do we think about sustainability when we buy fish? Look for the Marine Stewardship Council (MSC) blue label! Do we encourage our politicians to follow sustainable policies? Through our actions, do we point to the resurrection or to death through overuse?

9 Creation groaning

Romans 8:18–25

I (Margot) love autumn colour: for me, there is nothing better than walking in glorious golden woodland on a bright, crisp, sunny day. The colours are all a result of the breakdown of the leaves as they die away in preparation for the winter. So the wonderful colour, which seems so full of life, has death built into it.

Here we look at one of the classic passages used by those who seek a biblical approach to caring for the environment. Dropped into the middle of this famous chapter on faith is a significant statement about the state of creation and its future hope. We can imagine Paul pondering the natural world, with all its beauty but also with death and decay. The natural cycles of our world depend on death to sustain life, but this does not make it any less painful. Paul, in grappling with the suffering of this world, puts his hope in Christ and the future glory that Christ promises. Paul describes creation as groaning, bound in an endless cycle of decay. This bondage is not of its own making but is part of God's purpose in his plan for salvation – and there is good news: Christ has broken the power of sin and death through the cross so that creation can look toward a liberation from decay.

Suddenly we realise that the gospel is a whole lot bigger than we may have imagined. The power of the cross not only brings personal human redemption but also promises the end of death and pain for the whole of God's creation. Of course, we cannot interpret that promise within our own understanding of nature today: take away death and decay and we would soon have environmental collapse. The promise set before us is of a world transformed so that it can flourish in a completely new way.

The implications are enormous. If God has a redemption plan for the whole world, then the world cannot be seen simply as a stage on which the human drama of redemption is worked out. Nature is part of God's plan of redemption and our involvement in caring for the environment is therefore part of mission.

10 Held together in Christ

Colossians 1:15–23

For several years, I (Margot) worked as a university chaplain. One of the things that I found interesting was the number of physics students who were Christians. As they studied the complexity of the universe and the perfection of the mathematics supporting it, they clearly found it but a short step to belief in a Creator God.

In this passage, Paul is explaining the cosmic nature of Christ to Christians in Colossae. He argues that Christ was the agent of creation in the past and has an ongoing role in sustaining creation in the present and future. Christ has made peace for all creation through his sacrifice on the cross. The perfection of cosmic mathematics points to a perfect Redeemer holding creation together and bringing it to harmony.

But there is also a major challenge for Christians. Christ is both chief (firstborn) over all creation and the head of the church, which is his body. As members of the church, we should point towards these cosmic truths in the way we live as

Christians. We should work to bring peace to all creatures in God's world and to help nature and humanity find a restored relationship. This means that we need to think practically in the big and small decisions that we make in life. It is much easier to use disposable forks and plates for a church social, but does the waste produced point to a life-giving Saviour? It may be quicker to drive to church than to walk, but, if you are fit and mobile, do you really need to? Then what about the church boiler? Our own church was unable to find a sustainable option to replace an ailing oil-fired one, but we found the most economic boiler possible in an attempt to maximise efficiency. Many churches have found help through Eco Church, which provides a useful audit on the nuts and bolts of being the body of Christ in a creation-friendly way.

11 Creation made new

Revelation 21:1–5

Every so often, people come to us and say that there is no need to worry too much about caring for the earth because God promises to give us a completely new heaven and earth in the future. The word 'new' in Revelation 21:1, however, does not have that meaning. The Greek word is *kainos*, which means to be 'made new' or 'renewed'. It seems that God is into recycling. Far from being thrown into extinction like some cosmic paper plate, the new heaven and earth will be a redeemed and renewed form of our present heaven and earth.

It is impossible to know exactly what a renewed earth will look like. Revelation uses symbolic language to explain it further, saying that there will be no more 'sea' (v. 1). The sea is a symbol of chaos in Hebrew thought, and so its absence is symbolic of the end of the chaotic forces of evil. God dwells in the midst of his creation, and death and pain have been banished (v. 4). This passage echoes Isaiah 65:17 and the images there of a future harmony of creation. Whatever it looks like, it will be good!

The new creation is, however, not just about the future. The apostle Paul writes, 'If anyone is in Christ, the new creation has come' (2 Corinthians 5:17). As the body of Christ, we demonstrate the new creation now and point to the future when all creation will be made new. How does that look in practice?

A Rocha is a Christian environmental charity that seeks to bring God's love to all creation. Its first project (2001) in the UK was based in Southall, west London. In this intensely urban, inner-city area, their work is a parable of the glory that we hope for. When A Rocha UK started managing the project, it was an abandoned open space, marred by fly-tipping and covered in brambles. They worked to clean up the area to encourage wildlife and developed educational and leisure programmes to help local people connect with the natural world. Now, a rubbish-filled wasteland has become a haven for wildlife and a place for people to relax and enjoy the world of their Creator. In 2012 A Rocha UK acquired Wolf Fields, a three-acre site in Southall that had fallen into disrepair and was used only as a rubbish dump. Work started in 2013, and the site was developed as a community allotment and sensory garden. Creation still groans in Southall, but A Rocha UK has pointed towards the hope of liberation.

12 Our gospel hope

Romans 5:1–5

What is Christian hope? In October 2011, a small group of theologians, environmental activists and scientists gathered to discuss the issue in the light of the current environmental crisis. The meeting was convened by the John Ray Initiative and A Rocha. The delegates were all 'opinion formers' – people whom others look to when trying to make sense of the environment from a Christian perspective.

The group identified three types of hope. The first is the hope that the problems can be solved: regarding climate change, this was a popular position 20 years ago. We hoped that if the nations of the world all took action together, it would be possible to avert the worst effects of climate change. In 2011, and indeed now in 2020, this hope looks distinctly thin. The second sort of hope is the eschatological hope, which we have already discussed in our study of Revelation 21. This gives a firm hope for a wonderful future, but we need to also interpret it in the present. As a group, we came to examine a third form of hope – that of living our Christian hope while experiencing severe difficulties in our present life. We have come to call this 'resilient hope'.

Our present passage gives a clear exposition of this resilient Christian hope. It is based on our justification in Christ, which has restored our relationship with God. It looks to the future and the glory of God that will one day be revealed. It is not an otherworldly hope, however, but a tough reality that sustains us in the present. Paul speaks of a hope that comes out of suffering, that brings perseverance and strengthens character. The early church father Irenaeus believed that God uses suffering to strengthen Christians in their faith and life. Other Christians are wary of anything that might be seen to give a moral justification for suffering, but understand that suffering is a reality in our lives.

Christian hope is not dependent on easy circumstances, quick happy endings or health and prosperity. Most of us will struggle with personal sadness and pain during our lives. Our hope is that God is alongside us and that he works through our suffering. Our hope, shining through our weaknesses, points to the glory of the new creation, which is seen in each believer when we act out our resurrection hope in our daily lives.

3

Landscapes of promise

Our journey through life takes us through many different places and landscapes. Even if you have mostly lived in one place, you are likely to have had holidays in special landscapes: maybe by the sea or in the mountains. How do we respond to these unfamiliar landscapes? Are we in awe of snow-covered peaks? Do the stunning autumn colours of a maple forest cause us to wonder? Do we worry on stormy sea crossings? We can learn a lot about ourselves when the geography changes.

The Bible is full of different landscapes: mountains and deserts; hills and valleys; wilderness, forest, bush and pasture; river banks and shorelines. These are the places where the people of God lived out their faith and learned to follow him more fully. God used these different environments to teach his people different things and to draw them ever closer to him.

As we look at these biblical landscapes, we too can learn more about God and gain a new perspective on our own life journey. The landscapes are often metaphors for life circumstances and, as we step into them in our imaginations, we can see God working through them and discover a deeper understanding of our discipleship.

First published in *Bible Reflections for Older People*, January–April 2020.

1 This land

Deuteronomy 26:9

He brought us to this place and gave us this land, a land flowing with milk and honey.

The phrase 'a land flowing with milk and honey' has been taken into popular usage to mean a bounteous and wealthy land or country. Many people use the phrase to describe the United States.

In the Bible it is mentioned 20 times, and there the meaning is rather more specific. In this context milk means goat's milk, which is God telling the Israelites that they would be pastoralists on the hills and not growing crops in the valleys. Honey means bees, which were most likely to be found in the forests and wild places of the hills. One thing was certain: the land the Israelites were going to was very different to the rich, irrigated landscape of Egypt that they left behind. It would be a good land, but not the same as before.

Have you ever thought you were going to 'a land flowing with milk and honey', but when you got there found it was not quite what you expected? Maybe even now you are trying to adapt to a new situation. Or are you still searching for that land? Wherever you are and whatever your situation, ask God for his blessing.

PRAYER
Lord,
thank you for placing me where I am.
Show me how to make this place
a land flowing with milk and honey.
Amen

2 Forests

Psalm 96:12–13 (abridged)

Let all the trees of the forest sing for joy. Let all creation rejoice before the Lord, for he comes, he comes to judge the earth.

Springtime in woodland can seem magical. In the barrenness of winter, the forest floor is dark with mud and leaf litter, and the branches of the trees stick out like dead bones from the trunks. Then spring arrives: the first green shoots emerge through the leaf litter, followed by pretty woodland flowers. Then, as the spring birdsong strengthens, the tree branches burst open with delicate spring leaves. It truly seems that they sing for joy.

Getting older can seem like the winter of life. Hobbies, health and friendships can begin to wind down. But in life, as in nature, we can catch those glimpses of spring: not only snowdrops and crocuses and the lengthening days, but perhaps in holding a new baby or chatting to a young relative. These are special moments and, whatever they are and whenever they come, we should make sure we treasure them.

We might wonder why the psalmist says creation rejoices in God's coming judgement. It is because by judging the earth God will redeem and renew creation. Then all the trees of the forest will truly sing for joy and we will join the eternal song of heaven with them. Praise be!

PRAYER
Lord,
thank you for those moments of pure joy.
Help us to treasure them and keep our eyes fixed on you
and the joy of your redeeming love.
Amen

3 Lakes

Mark 4:39

[Jesus] got up, rebuked the wind and said to the waves, 'Quiet. Be still!' Then the wind died down and it was completely calm.

The Sea of Galilee is actually a relatively small lake, and it is possible to see across it. For much of the year it is calm, and in the summer it is hot and humid at the water's edge. But when storms do come they can be quite violent, even life-threatening.

When Jesus and the disciples took a boat trip from one side of the lake to the other, they got caught in such a storm. The disciples were terrified and went to wake Jesus, who was sleeping. With just three words, 'Quiet. Be still', the storm was pacified. The disciples were amazed that Jesus was able to do this. No wonder: it showed that Jesus was not only able to heal the sick, but had complete control over all aspects of the natural world.

At various times in our lives, we will know storms and rough seas. These may be illnesses, job losses or the deaths of loved ones. Maybe that is where we are right now, but Jesus will guide us through those storms and help us readjust when we reach a place of peace again. He will be with us both in the storms and in the calm that follows.

PRAYER
Lord,
we pray that you will be with us
both in the difficult times
and in the easier times that follow them.
Amen

4 Deserts

Exodus 16:2

In the desert the whole community grumbled against Moses and Aaron.

The Israelites were looking back with nostalgia. They were migrants on a long hike through a barren landscape, where food was sparse and the going was tough. They looked back to their time in Egypt, when they remembered plenty of food but forgot the forced labour and back-breaking hours. Here they were in freedom, with a new land ahead, yet they focused on the past and grumbled.

Sometimes life can feel a bit depressing, especially when we compare how things are now with how they were in the past. We may miss an exciting and prestigious job, or we may miss the times when family were all around. Maybe now, at times, we feel useless and lonely.

God was gentle in his response to the Israelites. He understood their tiredness and desperation. The story continues with the miracle of quail and manna from heaven. The Israelites did not know what manna was and would have missed it but for Moses showing them how to gather it. When life seems drab, it's tempting to look back with sadness. But resist that temptation and look instead for the signs of manna in life today. God might have some surprises in store.

PRAYER
Lord,
help me to see what you are doing in my life now.
Help me to give thanks for good things in the past
and to be confident of your loving care for me now.
Amen

5 Pastures

Psalm 23:1–2a

The Lord is my shepherd, I lack nothing. He makes me lie down in green pastures.

This is one of the most famous and best-loved psalms. Does it make you think of rolling English countryside, lush green grass, fluffy white sheep and a border collie sheepdog with a shepherd following behind? Of course, it was rather different in its original Middle Eastern context.

Throughout the Bible, the theme of sheep and shepherds is a strong one. This verse from Psalm 23 tells us three truths that recur again and again.

First, if we follow God we will lack nothing. This doesn't mean that we will always have all the material possessions that we want, but that we will have the spiritual resources to deal with any eventuality.

Second, we will 'lie down in green pastures', implying that the shepherd will find the perfect place for us. Again, we might not think it is the perfect place, but the shepherd always knows what is best for us.

But who is the shepherd? Jesus said of himself, 'I am the good shepherd. The good shepherd lays down his life for the sheep' (John 10:11). So, third, we can be assured that Jesus is the good shepherd and that he will look after us. All we need to do is to trust in him.

PRAYER
Lord,
I thank you that you are the good shepherd.
Show me how to be a good sheep.
Amen

6 The sea

Jonah 2:2

'In my distress I called to the Lord, and he answered me. From deep in the realm of the dead I called for help, and you listened to my cry.'

It was just before Christmas. We'd both been out for the day and came home feeling lousy. Before we knew it, we were in bed experiencing the worst flu that we'd ever known. Being in a vicarage, this had some special challenges in terms of progressively finding others to cover all the Christmas services, but also some amazing blessings, with food appearing on the doorstep and many other kindnesses. We truly had a wonderful team.

We never know when the storms of life will hit us, and our flu was very minor compared to life's fiercer storms, such as life-changing illness, tragedy and bereavement. We can feel lost and abandoned by God at these times.

Jonah had been going his own way in life when tragedy hit, and he might easily have thought that all was lost. But instead, he turned to prayer.

We won't all have the miraculous rescue that Jonah had, but we can all trust in God, who cares for us and brings us salvation. When we're in a difficult situation and pray, something changes. Sometimes the situation changes, but even if it doesn't, something inside us changes so we begin to see the situation differently. We might want to pray for ourselves or for someone else. Whoever our prayer is for, we can trust God.

PRAYER

Lord,
help us to pray in all of life's circumstances.
Show us your perspective
and help us to trust you more.
Amen

7 Wilderness

Isaiah 35:1–2a

The desert and the parched land will be glad; the wilderness
will rejoice and blossom. Like the crocus, it will burst into bloom;
it will rejoice greatly and shout for joy.

A friend once went camping in the dry and rocky Negev desert in Israel, during a period of rain. One morning, he woke to find that he was surrounded by a carpet of flowers. It was stunningly beautiful and he dared not move in case he trod on the flowers. Desert flower seeds can lie dormant in the ground for many years, leaving the landscape looking completely barren, but as soon as it rains the seeds germinate and the flowers bloom.

Sometimes we have gifts and talents that can lie dormant, especially through the busy years when juggling work and family takes up all our time. For some, retirement can look like a barren landscape, but this is when more spare time can be like gentle rain on the seeds of half-forgotten talents and interests, allowing them to flourish once again, or even for the first time.

Gifts and talents can be discovered – or rediscovered – and shared, bringing new vibrancy and colour to life in retirement. It's also a good time to refresh your relationship with God. If he can bring flowers to the desert, there is no telling what he can do in our lives.

PRAYER

Thank you, Lord, for the gift of time.
Show me how to use this precious gift
and lead me more deeply into your presence.
Amen

8   Rivers

Psalm 137:1

By the rivers of Babylon we sat and wept when we remembered Zion.

The song 'Rivers of Babylon' was popularised by the group Boney M. in the 1970s and is one of the few pop songs to use words from the Bible. The passage from Psalm 137 refers to when the Jewish people were taken into exile in Babylon. It was a time of deep national trauma and reflection, and we can imagine the Israelites sitting on the banks of the Tigris and Euphrates rivers, looking back on the time they were in Judah and regretting all the things they had done wrong. They had ignored the warnings of their prophets and had paid the price. Now, they found themselves in captivity and in the unfamiliar land of Babylon. Inevitably, the tears came.

Hopefully, none of us will ever be in a situation as serious as the Babylonian exile. But it is quite possible that we find ourselves in unfamiliar surroundings today, or will do in the future. How do we react? A sense of loss and longing is surely only natural, but perhaps we shouldn't put all of the focus on ourselves.

There are now millions of refugees living in temporary accommodation in unfamiliar landscapes around the world. Many will have very similar feelings to the Israelites in Babylon. Let's remember them now.

PRAYER
Loving God,
be with all those who have moved home recently,
whether by choice or out of necessity.
Comfort, protect and encourage them
in their new surroundings.
Amen

9 Mountains

Mark 9:2

Jesus took Peter, James and John with him and led them up a high mountain, where they were all alone. There he was transfigured before them.

We often hear people talking about 'mountaintop experiences': those special times with God. Peter, James and John certainly had one of those moments. As Jesus led them up Mount Hermon, his garments shone brightly, and suddenly Moses and Elijah appeared from nowhere. Then a voice from a cloud said, 'This is my Son, whom I love. Listen to him!' before things returned to normal. This was not at all a typical hike up a mountain.

But what happened next? Mark's gospel tells us that Jesus led the three disciples down the mountain, and he was soon back among the people, healing a boy who had an impure spirit. So the mountaintop experience didn't last forever, and they were soon back to work.

And so it is for us. We love, even crave, those experiences at the top of the mountain, but they're not a permanent state. God intends that we should all benefit from these experiences, but that we should then come down from the mountain to do his work. The mountaintop is where we hear and see God, but the valleys are where we live out our lives, serving God in the day-to-day.

PRAYER
Lord,
if it is your will,
give us a mountaintop experience.
But also show us how to live
in the valley below.
Amen

10 Caring for the land

Deuteronomy 20:19 (abridged)

When you lay siege to a city for a long time... do not destroy its trees by putting an axe to them, because you can eat their fruit... Are the trees people, that you should besiege them?

Is it worth sacrificing everything to win? As a young person, it can seem so, and over time sacrifices might be regained. With maturity, we realise that few prizes are worth destroying everything else for and, ultimately, family, friends and community are those things of greatest value.

Sometimes armies have destroyed farms, woodland and orchards in battle, only to discover the cost of their loss after victory. This passage looks at the specific issue of armies cutting down orchards, but has a wider application for our care of nature as a whole. It can be seen in two ways: first, we should care for creation because we depend on it for life. If we destroy our planet, we destroy ourselves. But second, we should care for nature because it is an innocent bystander in the drama of human activity. It does not lay siege to us and so we should protect it.

In the end, we have to ask whether the goal of continuing economic growth is worth the cost of damaging God's earth beyond immediate repair. As people with the wisdom of age, we have something important to contribute in this debate.

PRAYER
Dear Lord,
help us to value your creation
and care for it more effectively.
Amen

4

Sharing resources

The early church knew a lot about how to share resources. Soon after the Day of Pentecost we read in Acts 2:44–45: 'All the believers were together and had everything in common. They sold property and possessions to give to anyone who had need.' Right from the beginning, the church was intended to be a sharing community. Sadly, it has not always lived up to that calling.

The next ten reflections are not all necessarily obviously 'green', although some are. But in many respects if we are sharing resources and using them wisely, we cannot help but be environmentally friendly. Of course, the early church did not have to think too much about sharing resources with the other residents of planet Earth. But in the 21st century, we certainly do. As we shall see we need to, 'leave a bit at the edge of our fields for our rabbits!'

First published in *Holy Habits Bible Reflections: Sharing Resources* (BRF, 2020).

1 Stewardship

Genesis 1:28–30

God blessed them and said to them, 'Be fruitful and increase in number; fill the earth and subdue it. Rule over the fish in the sea and the birds in the sky and over every living creature that moves on the ground.' Then God said, 'I give you every seed-bearing plant on the face of the whole earth and every tree that has fruit with seed in it. They will be yours for food. And to all the beasts of the earth and all the birds in the sky and all the creatures that move along the ground – everything that has the breath of life in it – I give every green plant for food.' And it was so.

How should we relate to nature? The command to 'fill the earth and subdue it' is controversial. In the King James Version, our passage reads, 'Have dominion over the fish…' Words like subdue and dominion can seem very harsh, and down the ages people, including Christians, have used passages like this as excuses to do what they like with creation. Famously, in 1967, this led American historian Lynn White Jr to state that 'Christianity is the most anthropocentric religion the world has seen'.

Since White launched his attack, biblical scholars have looked more closely at the Hebrew words in this passage. It seems that the word used for 'subdue' is possibly a ploughing metaphor, which suggests aiding the fruitfulness of the land rather than treading it down. The word we translate 'dominion' or 'rule' is the same word as that used by King Solomon in his just reign over Israel. So the original Hebrew meaning of the passage was almost certainly not as harsh as it has often been interpreted. In fact, this passage has more recently been used to support a positive ethical view.

White's attack on Christianity and its attitude to the natural world set in motion a whole train of thinking and stimulated the development of environmental ethics and theology. Our passage and others like it were used to develop the concept of stewardship, the idea that humans are responsible for the world and should take care of it. But stewardship soon went beyond thinking about the natural world. It is now often applied to money and in financial and business affairs. If we are thinking about how we share our resources, then we are really thinking about stewardship.

Lord God, give me wisdom as we look at the topic of sharing resources in this series. Amen

2 Hospitality

Genesis 18:1–5

The Lord appeared to Abraham near the great trees of Mamre while he was sitting at the entrance to his tent in the heat of the day. Abraham looked up and saw three men standing nearby. When he saw them, he hurried from the entrance of his tent to meet them and bowed low to the ground. He said, 'If I have found favour in your eyes, my lord, do not pass your servant by. Let a little water be brought, and then you may all wash your feet and rest under this tree. Let me get you something to eat, so you can be refreshed and then go on your way – now that you have come to your servant.' 'Very well,' they answered, 'do as you say.'

Genesis 18 opens in a somewhat mysterious way, when three men appear to Abraham as he rested at the entrance of his tent on a hot day. Abraham somehow recognises that one of them is the Lord (the other two may have been angels) and immediately offers them hospitality, first water to drink and to wash their feet and later a meal. This kind of hospitality was, and still is, typical of that found in the Middle East. The New Testament church was also very much built on hospitality and takes up this theme in 1 Peter 4:9: 'Offer hospitality to one another without grumbling.'

Years ago, I (Martin) was between houses and staying in a small bedsit until a house purchase went through six weeks later. There were no cooking facilities. I was working at Birmingham University and so food was no problem in the week, and I spied out the fish and chip shop for Sunday lunch. But I also spotted the small local church and went there on my first Sunday. After the service, at coffee, an older couple came up to me, recognising that I was new. Would I like lunch? When I got to their house, they had lots of guests for lunch. They had food on the go every week, never knowing who the guests would be! When I explained my situation, they fixed me up with Sunday lunch every week with a different church family. I never needed the chip shop. Whenever I hear the word 'hospitality', it always takes me back to that small church.

Sharing hospitality, especially food, is a key biblical principle. It is perhaps not surprising that many modern church initiatives (e.g. Alpha and Messy Church) also involve sharing a meal together.

Lord, give me opportunities to help my church develop its ministry of hospitality. Amen

3 Tithing

Deuteronomy 14:22–23, 28–29

Be sure to set aside a tenth of all that your fields produce each year. Eat the tithe of your corn, new wine and olive oil, and the firstborn of your herds and flocks in the presence of the Lord your God at the place he will choose as a dwelling for his Name, so that you may learn to revere the Lord your God always... At the end of every three years, bring all the tithes of that year's produce and store it in your towns, so that the Levites (who have no land allotted to them or inheritance of their own) and the foreigners, the fatherless and the widows who live in your towns may come and eat and be satisfied, and so that the Lord your God may bless you in all the work of your hands.

From the first part of this passage, it is clear that the original command to the Jewish people concerning tithing suggested that they should put aside a tenth of their agricultural produce each year and then eat it in a place chosen by God. In the second section, we see that every three years tithes were to be used to support the Levites who worked at the temple and the poor and vulnerable.

Throughout the Old Testament, tithing is a strong theme, and this is carried over into the New Testament when Jesus states, 'Woe to you, teachers of the law and

Pharisees, you hypocrites! You give a tenth of your spices – mint, dill and cumin. But you have neglected the more important matters of the law – justice, mercy and faithfulness. You should have practised the latter, without neglecting the former' (Matthew 23:23).

Throughout history, churches have had various regulations concerning tithing, some voluntary and some compulsory. Most gifts are now in the form of money. But how do we decide where our money should go? Clearly the provision for the Levites gives a strong precedent for the support of the church and its ministers, and without our support the institutions would flounder and our clergy would not be able to undertake full-time ministry.

However, Jesus makes it evident that giving should come from the heart and not just be a mechanical process. So 'justice, mercy and faithfulness' also come into tithing. There are very many worthy charities working with the poor and homeless that could really do with our help. We need to prayerfully consider where we place our giving. Many Christians give a certain percentage to their church, and the rest to the charities they particularly support. Maybe that could be a way forward for you?

Lord, show me how to apportion my giving. Amen

4 Justice

Deuteronomy 15:1–5

At the end of every seven years you must cancel debts. This is how it is to be done: every creditor shall cancel any loan they have made to a fellow Israelite. They shall not require payment from anyone among their own people, because the Lord's time for cancelling debts has been proclaimed. You may require payment from a foreigner, but you must cancel any debt your fellow Israelite owes you. However, there need be no poor people among you, for in the land the Lord your God is giving you to possess as your inheritance, he will richly bless you, if only you fully obey the Lord your God and are careful to follow all these commands I am giving you today.

The premise that every seven years the Israelites should cancel their debts is related to the idea of sabbath, as expressed in Genesis 2:2, when God rested from his creative activity. This is then extended to giving the land a sabbath: 'During the seventh year let the land lie unploughed and unused' (Exodus 23:11). In carrying out this command, the Israelites would in effect be repaying their debt to the land and giving it a rest. Our passage today extends this idea to the people. They should be free of debt, and God intended that there should be no poor people among them. Paul has this to say about debt: 'Let no debt remain outstanding, except the continuing debt to love one another, for whoever loves others has fulfilled the law' (Romans 13:8).

Despite all these good intentions, people are still in debt, as indeed are whole countries. Although there are fewer poor people in the world now than at the turn of the millennium, globally inequality has grown, with a few very rich people having more wealth than millions of poor people. As our passage and many others in the Bible make clear, God is a God of justice, and he cares about the poor and those who are in debt.

Throughout history, Christians have taken up this theme, trying to 'transform unjust structures of society', as the fourth of the Anglican marks of mission puts it. Jubilee 2000 sought to relieve poor countries of crippling debts which prevented them from developing. More recent campaigns include Drop the Debt and Make Poverty History. In all these cases, Christians were very much involved, often taking leading positions. How can we help? We can give assistance to finance organisations working in this area, we can write to our politicians and we can get directly involved in this work as individuals and as churches.

God of justice, how can I help 'transform unjust structures of society'?

5 Generosity

Deuteronomy 15:7–10

If anyone is poor among your fellow Israelites in any of the towns of the land that the Lord your God is giving you, do not be hard-hearted or tight-fisted towards them. Rather, be openhanded and freely lend them whatever they need. Be careful not to harbour this wicked thought: 'The seventh year, the year for cancelling debts, is near,' so that you do not show ill will towards the needy among your fellow Israelites and give them nothing. They may then appeal to the Lord against you, and you will be found guilty of sin. Give generously to them and do so without a grudging heart; then because of this the Lord your God will bless you in all your work and in everything you put your hand to.

Although our previous passage suggested that the ideal was that there would be no poor people in Israel, God is realistic and knows that there will be. So how are we to treat these people? Here and throughout the Bible, we are instructed to give generously. But how this should be done raises all sorts of issues. Jesus gives this advice: 'But when you give to the needy, do not let your left hand know what your right hand is doing, so that your giving may be in secret. Then your Father, who sees what is done in secret, will reward you' (Matthew 6:3–4). It is clear that we should not be making a lot of our giving, and preferably this should be done in secret.

But what do we do today when we pass someone begging in the street? There are two main approaches. We could stop and give the person some money directly. The disadvantage of this is that we do not know what the money will be used for. Giving money can exacerbate any problems with addiction, which interact with homelessness. The other route is to give money to organisations that are working with the beggars and the homeless. These will have specialist knowledge and will be able to ensure that any money given is well used. It still feels hard, though, walking past people. It may be that different approaches are appropriate depending on the circumstances. The most important thing is to acknowledge people, to say hello and maybe offer some food. Some homeless shelters offer tokens that people can buy to give out. Whatever route we eventually decide to take, we should 'not show ill will towards the needy' and give generously to those less well off than ourselves.

Lord, give me a spirit of generosity. Amen

6 Gleaning

Deuteronomy 24:19–22

When you are harvesting in your field and you overlook a sheaf, do not go back to get it. Leave it for the foreigner, the fatherless and the widow, so that the Lord your God may bless you in all the work of your hands. When you beat the olives from your trees, do not go over the branches a second time. Leave what remains for the foreigner, the fatherless and the widow. When you harvest the grapes in your vineyard, do not go over the vines again. Leave what remains for the foreigner, the fatherless and the widow. Remember that you were slaves in Egypt. That is why I command you to do this.

Years ago, an old Cotswold farmer was asked why he did not shoot the rabbits in his wheat field. His response was that he harvested 90% of the wheat and he left the rest to his rabbits. He may or may not have realised it, but he was following a biblical principle, in that he was allowing the rabbits to glean his fields.

In the Bible, gleaning is the collection of grain, grapes and other crops left behind after the main harvest. So the Cotswold farmer was even more generous, as he didn't mind his rabbits gathering some of the wheat even before it was harvested. Gleaning was intended to be kind to poor people and to foreigners. Our passage calls on the Jewish people to 'remember that you were slaves in Egypt' and to do justice.

Perhaps the most famous story of gleaning in the Bible concerns Ruth the Moabite (Ruth 2). Ruth and Naomi were almost certainly very hungry after a long journey from Moab to Israel, so Ruth went gleaning barley in a field. There she met the owner of the field, Boaz, who was very kind to her and eventually married her. And so Ruth the Moabite became the great-grandmother of King David.

Where do we see the principle of gleaning being applied today? It is still best seen in an agricultural context. For many years now, farmers have been able to apply for Environmental Stewardship schemes in the UK. These help nature to flourish by careful management practices. So we often see wild flower strips around the edges of fields. The farmers allow nature to glean from their fields and share their resources with the rich biodiversity that can develop. In return, the insects resident in the strips often help protect the fields against pests.

How might you apply the principle of gleaning in your life?

Dear God, show me how to leave a little of my bounty for other people and/or other creatures. Amen

7 Food

1 Kings 17:13–16

Elijah said to her, 'Don't be afraid. Go home and do as you have said. But first make a small loaf of bread for me from what you have and bring it to me, and then make something for yourself and your son. For this is what the Lord, the God of Israel, says: "The jar of flour will not be used up and the jug of oil will not run dry until the day the Lord sends rain on the land."' She went away and did as Elijah had told her. So there was food every day for Elijah and for the woman and her family. For the jar of flour was not used up and the jug of oil did not run dry, in keeping with the word of the Lord spoken by Elijah.

The story of Elijah and the widow at Zarephath takes place in the context of a severe drought in Israel which lasted for several years. After being fed by the ravens, Elijah was instructed by God to go to Zarephath, where a widow would give him food. When he arrived there, he found her gathering sticks to make a fire. She intended to use her last remaining flour and oil to make a meal for her and her son before they both died from starvation. Elijah asked God for a miracle that would keep himself, the widow and her son in bread and oil until the end of the famine. This is the first miracle involving multiplication of food recorded in the Bible.

There are many places in the world where people are going hungry today. Sadly, there are now many in the United Kingdom who do not have enough food to eat. The response of the churches across the country has been amazing, with many involved in setting up food banks. Between 1 April 2019 and 31 March 2020, Trussell Trust food banks distributed 1.9 million three-day emergency food supplies to people in crisis, from 1,200 food banks around the UK. In April 2020 there was an 89 per cent surge in demand as the Covid-19 lockdown began. Families with children are those most likely to need food banks, and there are many reports in the media of children going without food.

What can we do about this crisis? How can we share our resources? Food banks are always looking for volunteers. Churches can set up or help run food banks in more deprived areas. In well-off areas, food can be collected and taken to towns and cities where the need is greater. Be careful to be on the lookout for food poverty, even in places that appear to be wealthy. And pray.

Lord, show me how I can help the hungry in my community. Amen

8 Interest

2 Kings 4:1–3

The wife of a man from the company of the prophets cried out to Elisha, 'Your servant my husband is dead, and you know that he revered the Lord. But now his creditor is coming to take my two boys as his slaves.' Elisha replied to her, 'How can I help you? Tell me, what do you have in your house?' 'Your servant has nothing there at all,' she said, 'except a small jar of olive oil.' Elisha said, 'Go round and ask all your neighbours for empty jars. Don't ask for just a few.'

The Bible is not keen on the charging of interest on loans. God does not like debt and wants to help people that are in such trouble. In today's passage, we hear the story of a woman whose husband has recently died, and his creditors are threatening to take her sons into slavery if she does not pay off his debts. Elisha asks her what she owns, and she says she just has one small jar of olive oil. The prophet says she should ask her neighbours for more empty jars. She should then pour oil into them. The oil from the one small jar filled many others – a miracle! The woman then sold the oil and was able to pay off her debts.

Throughout history, loans for interest have been controversial and often criticised. According to the Jewish commentator Rashi, the Hebrew word for 'bite' has the same root as the word for 'interest': 'It resembles the bite of a snake… inflicting a small wound in a person's foot which he does not feel at first, but all at once it swells, and distends the whole body up to the top of his head. So it is with interest.'

Today, people still get into debt and struggle with high-interest payments. In 2013, Archbishop of Canterbury Justin Welby launched an attack on the payday loan companies operating in the UK. These companies were charging very high interest rates, and desperate people were trapped in a cycle of debt. Three years later, tougher regulations forced many of the companies out of business, but debt remains a very serious problem. Many churches have responded to the debt crisis by setting up schemes to give monetary advice. Often there are people in their congregations who are real experts in financial affairs who are willing to help.

Lord God, I pray for all those trapped in debt. Show me how I might be able to help. Amen

9 Famine

2 Kings 4:38–41

Elisha returned to Gilgal and there was a famine in that region. While the company of the prophets was meeting with him, he said to his servant, 'Put on the large pot and cook some stew for these prophets.' One of them went out into the fields to gather herbs and found a wild gourd plant and picked as many of its gourds as his garment could hold. When he returned, he cut them up into the pot of stew, though no one knew what they were. The stew was poured out for the men, but as they began to eat it, they cried out, 'Man of God, there is death in the pot!' And they could not eat it. Elisha said, 'Get some flour.' He put it into the pot and said, 'Serve it to the people to eat.' And there was nothing harmful in the pot.

This is a rather mysterious story! In the midst of a famine, Elisha was trying to be hospitable to a group of prophets that had gathered around him. He sent his servant off to find some vegetables. The servant spotted a wild vine and grabbed as many of its gourds as he could carry. What exactly was the gourd plant? It seems that it was colocynth (*Citrullus colocynthis*), a vine that trails along the sand in the desert near the Dead Sea. The plant is used in traditional medicines, including as a laxative, but it is toxic and potentially fatal. Colocynth was said to have been used by Agrippina to poison her husband, the Roman Emperor Claudius, in AD54. Not surprisingly, the bitter taste of the stew, and some of the early symptoms of eating a small amount of it, provoked a negative reaction from the prophets: 'There is death in the pot!' Elisha solved the problem by adding flour to the stew. This would surely have decreased the bitter taste, but why the stew suddenly lost its toxicity is not certain. Maybe it was a miracle?

Hunger and famine are still major problems. The second of the sustainable development goals, set by the United Nations in 2015, is 'zero hunger'. The UN estimated that 815 million people were undernourished, mostly in poor countries. The ambitious aim is that by 2030 nobody should be hungry. Reaching this target at a time of rapid population growth, climate change and biodiversity loss, and without wrecking our agricultural soils, will be a major challenge. That challenge has undoubtedly been made more difficult by the Covid-19 pandemic. Only a few people will have the necessary skills to help the United Nations achieve this laudable goal in a direct way. But there are many secular and Christian charities that are working in this area. You could support one or more of these as an individual and encourage your church to do the same.

Lord Jesus, I pray that there will soon come a time when nobody in the world goes hungry. Amen

10 Compassion

Exodus 22:25–27

If you lend money to one of my people among you who is needy, do not treat it like a business deal; charge no interest. If you take your neighbour's cloak as a pledge, return it by sunset, because that cloak is the only covering your neighbour has. What else can they sleep in? When they cry out to me, I will hear, for I am compassionate.

If a person got into debt, the Jewish law said that under some circumstances they could make a pledge. So in our present passage, a person gets into debt to a neighbour and loses his cloak as a pledge or surety. But because the person is poor, the neighbour is supposed to return it to him every night to sleep in. In practice, continually having to pick up the cloak in the morning and return it in the evening would probably have put the neighbour off doing so. God is a God of mercy and compassion and listens to the cries of the people, particularly the poor.

Neil deGrasse Tyson, the American scientist and media personality, once said, 'For me, I am driven by two main philosophies: know more today about the world than I knew yesterday and lessen the suffering of others. You'd be surprised how far that gets you.' As a scientist, it is Tyson's job to increase our knowledge of the world. But it is all of our jobs to be compassionate and to lessen suffering. How are we to do that? We have seen that there are many ways we can help. We can carefully consider the stewardship of our financial resources, and help others with how they look after money. We can offer hospitality. We can support charities that help with the homeless on our streets, help to feed the hungry both close to home and across the world, and fight against injustice wherever we see it. And don't forget that we need to share our resources with the rest of creation – leave a bit at the edge of our fields for our rabbits!

Pray for wisdom. God says, 'I will hear, for I am compassionate.' Amen

5

Storms and fair weather

'It looks like rain today.' The British love talking about the weather. Will it rain? Will it stop? Is it a good summer or a hard winter? We all have an opinion. Weather affects people's moods, and they are noticeably more cheerful when it is sunny (but not too hot) and are more irritable when it is wet or cold. Climate change is affecting our weather and causes anxiety, especially to young people.

The Bible is full of weather. Through different weather, God's people learned how to depend on him and how to follow him in all circumstances. The Middle East is very dry, and rain became a metaphor for God's blessing. At times of drought, people prayed for rain, and they also turned to God to work more fully in their lives as they realised how far they had drifted from him.

'It's brightening up a bit' is an optimistic British weather phrase. The rain might be lashing on the windows, but with a slight lightening of the sky we look for sunshine. We hope these reflections guide you to see the brightening hand of God working in your life, through storms and fair weather, to lead you to know him better.

First published in *Bible Reflections for Older People*, January–April 2021.

1 Well prepared

Proverbs 31:21

When it snows, she has no fear for her household; for all of them are clothed in scarlet.

Snow is beautiful, but it is often inconvenient. If you need to get about for whatever reason, it can be hazardous, and many people will fear a serious fall and its consequences. But if you are active and have the right footwear, with a suitable place to take a walk on a sunny, snowy day, it is a magical experience. Looking at a snow scene through a window, while safe in the warmth, can also bring back happy memories of snowball fights and snowmen of old.

Snow is not often expected in Israel, but the woman in Proverbs 31 is very organised. When bad weather comes, she is able to handle it. She runs a big household, is raising a family and even manages a farm, but she is so well prepared that everyone is looked after. Being responsible for other people and managing responsibilities at home and at work can be a real juggling act, and it takes special skill to be prepared when the unexpected happens. But even when those days of responsibility are behind us, building a regular time to pray enables us to be prepared for all weathers and for all that life brings us. Instead of panicking, we can calmly bring our concerns to God, and he will show us a way forward.

PRAYER

Dear Lord,
help me to rely on you day by day,
so that you prepare me to be calm and trusting,
whatever the weather.
Amen

2 Rain in season

Leviticus 26:4

I will send you rain in its season, and the ground will yield its crops
and the trees their fruit.

I (Margot) love the seasons, and, as each one comes on the horizon, I look forward to the changes in the countryside: the primroses and fresh leaves of spring;
summer's colour with long, warm days, or dashing undercover from unexpected
rain; crunching through autumn leaves with the glorious golden display on the
trees; and even winter, for all its cold and rain, has its special moments when the
snow falls and the world stands still.

Now I notice that the seasons are changing. Spring is a little earlier, with bluebells
coming out in April rather than May. Golden October is becoming golden November.
The summer is more often hotter and drier or much wetter than in years gone by,
and the winter is warmer but stormier. In other parts of the world, these changes
have led to crop failures when the rains come at the wrong times – or don't come at
all – and older people lose their role advising on the best time to plant or harvest.

As our climate changes, it is important to remember that the earth is the Lord's (Psalm 24:1) and that we have a responsibility to care for all he has made. Even small changes, like moving to a renewable energy tariff, not wasting food and other resources, repairing and recycling, will help to secure the seasons' rhythm for future generations.

PRAYER
Lord,
give us courage to change where we need to
and to care for your creation entrusted to us.
Amen

3 Tossed by the wind

James 1:6

But when you ask, you must believe and not doubt, because the one who doubts is like a wave of the sea, blown and tossed by the wind.

I (Margot) love sailing but am not an expert. I once got caught in a tidal estuary and was unable to get back to land. However hard my friend and I tried, every small progress was thwarted by the current pushing us back out to sea. We eventually became exhausted and were humble enough to say 'Yes!' when the skipper of a passing motorboat asked us if we needed help. He tossed us a line and towed us into harbour. I clung to that rope for dear life, and I have never felt so relieved to reach dry land.

The apostle James was writing to people who faced difficult situations. They needed wisdom to make decisions and the courage to see them through. Sometimes we know the right decision, but seeing it through can seem like trying to sail a boat against the tide. Prayer is our lifeline, and if we persevere we will find that God will give us strength to face the wind and the waves of difficulties. He will lead us into safe havens.

PRAYER
Lord,
give us strength to keep going
when things get difficult.
Give us wisdom to make courageous decisions
when we know they are right.
Give us humility to ask for your help
when the going gets tough.
Amen

4 Going under

Psalm 69:15

Do not let the floodwaters engulf me or the depths swallow me up or the pit close its mouth over me.

Psalm 69 is attributed to King David, a man who knew many ups and downs in his life. Four verses in the psalm refer to flooding or drowning, suggesting that the writer had some knowledge of this kind of event. Israel is an arid country, but David spent time in the wadis around the Dead Sea while he was hiding as a fugitive from King Saul. For most of the year these are dry, but then rains in the Jerusalem area can rapidly turn the wadis into raging torrents. It is easy for the unwary to be trapped in the wadi, unable to escape as the flood waters rise.

The winter of 2019/20 in the United Kingdom was both the fifth wettest in recorded history and the fifth mildest. The heavy rain caused widespread flooding and considerable damage to property. Homeowners often cleaned up after one flood, only for the waters to return a few weeks later. But we are fortunate in being a rich country with good forecasting and emergency services. Many in poor countries are much less lucky.

PRAYER
Pray for those affected by severe weather events, both in the United Kingdom and abroad. Pray too for those trying to bring relief to those affected.

5 When the storm subsides

Genesis 9:28

After the flood Noah lived 350 years.

Noah's ark is one of the best-known stories in the Bible. Following God's call, Noah builds an ark and saves pairs of every animal and his own family, as a terrible flood wipes out the rest of life. We know Noah the hero, but what happened next?

Noah lived another 350 years, and those years were not without their challenges. A modern reader might wonder if he suffered post-traumatic stress disorder (PTSD) after the trauma of the flood. Might that have led to a sad episode when he became drunk on wine from his vineyard? Or did he simply find it very difficult to settle down to a humdrum life, after such a courageous time? He was fortunate to have sons who came to his aid.

Roles with major responsibility, respect and sometimes fame usually come around the middle of our lives. It can be hard to accept a more ordinary life afterwards, and we can yearn for the days when 'we were somebody'. But when we turn to God, we find that we are infinitely valuable to him, whatever our role or stage in life. He loves us not for what we are, but for who we are. Moreover, he can guide us in how to spend our gift of years to enrich the lives of others as well as our own.

PRAYER
Thank you, Lord,
for giving me the gift of years.
Help me to use these years wisely and joyfully.
Amen.

6 A dry and thirsty land

Deuteronomy 8:15

He led you through the vast and dreadful wilderness, that thirsty and waterless land, with its venomous snakes and scorpions. He brought you water out of hard rock.

After their escape from Egypt, God led the Israelites into the wilderness for 40 years before they entered the promised land. The Sinai Desert is a dry, inhospitable land. There were miracles along the way, like the manna which God sent to feed them, but overall it must have been a difficult time for the people. God tested them and built them into a nation, so that they would be ready for what lay ahead in Israel.

Before Jesus began his public ministry, he was also tested in the wilderness, but this time for 40 days and 40 nights. The number 40 is special in Jewish thought, appearing in many places in the Bible and suggesting the period between two epochs or a very long time period.

Sometimes life can be quite a test, and it can feel as if we are wandering in a wilderness. It may be illness, the loss of a job or bereavement, or we may feel lonely and unwanted. God can seem very distant in these wilderness days, but remembering Jesus' words, 'And surely I am with you always, to the very end of the age' (Matthew 28:20) can really help us get through them.

PRAYER
Lord Jesus,
we pray that you will be with us
through all of the trials of life.
Amen

7 Stormy weather

Jeremiah 51:16

When he thunders, the waters in the heavens roar; he makes clouds rise from the ends of the earth. He sends lightning with the rain and brings out the wind from his storehouses.

In February 2020 the Swedish climate activist Greta Thunberg came to Bristol to lead a climate strike by the young people of the city and the surrounding area. The city ground to a standstill, and over 25,000 people came, despite the pouring rain.

The 'waters in the heavens' really did roar, and everyone was soaked. Greta, in typical style, told the crowd, 'Our leaders behave like children so it falls to us to be the adults in the room. They are failing us, but we will not back down.'

Like Jeremiah all those years ago, Greta is a prophet. Jeremiah spoke to the people of Israel in Babylon, who were exiled for disobeying God. Greta speaks for her generation against the rich and the powerful. Millions of young people all around the world have joined the climate strike movement as the effects of climate change become ever more obvious. Maybe you know some of the youth and children that have been involved. Maybe you also know some young people who are suffering from anxiety about climate change or having nightmares. Remember them now.

PRAYER
Lord,
we pray for all the young people raising the alarm on climate change
and for those who are frightened by it.
We also pray for world leaders,
that they will take notice.
Amen

8 Red sky at night

Matthew 16:2–3

[Jesus] replied, 'When evening comes, you say, "It will be fair weather, for the sky is red," and in the morning, "Today it will be stormy, for the sky is red and overcast." You know how to interpret the appearance of the sky, but you cannot interpret the signs of the times.'

'Red sky at night, shepherd's delight. Red sky in the morning, shepherd's warning.' It may surprise you to know that this old saying has its origins in the Bible. The Pharisees and Sadducees had come to Jesus, asking him to give them a sign that he was the Messiah. He replied that they knew how to interpret the weather signs, but not the signs of the times. Jesus had already performed many miracles, and it was already clear that he was special.

One of the advantages of age and experience is that we can more easily interpret the signs of our times, or at least we should be able to.

Wisdom can take a long time coming. It can be a very long time before we come to realise that Jesus is the Messiah, the anointed one, and the Son of God. But it is never too late. If you have never before recognised that Jesus is the Messiah, ask him to come into your life. Or maybe you have known Jesus for many years, but long for a family member or friend to come to know him. Pray for them.

PRAYER
Lord,
I pray that you will come into my life
and into the lives of my family and friends.
Amen

9 Bring me sunshine

Proverbs 4:18

The path of the righteous is like the morning sun, shining ever brighter till the full light of day.

There are three people whom I (Margot) remember as teenagers, who are now well-known Christian leaders. I remember them as young people with a thriving faith, a passion for ethical principles and vision in their eyes.

It is good to see how their lives have grown and blossomed. They all now carry big responsibilities, have all had to face major challenges and have each made a major difference in the church and wider world. In many ways, they are shining stars among the people I know.

But there are others I remember who have also 'shone brighter' as their lives have progressed. They have not become well known, but they have lived their lives faithfully and well, bringing up families, making thoughtful career choices and becoming backbones of their local churches and communities.

We all have the opportunity to make sunshine in this world. It leads some people to take up major and high-profile roles, but for most people making sunshine is about living our lives well: honestly, faithfully and conscientiously and, when we have made mistakes, being willing to admit them.

When we next see the sunrise, let's ask God to give us a fresh opportunity to share his love and make sunshine.

PRAYER
Lord,
give us a vision for where we might bring light
and hope to those around us.
Amen

10 In a whisper

1 Kings 19:11b–12

Then a great and powerful wind tore the mountains apart and shattered the rocks before the Lord, but the Lord was not in the wind. After the wind there was an earthquake, but the Lord was not in the earthquake. After the earthquake came a fire, but the Lord was not in the fire. And after the fire came a gentle whisper.

Elijah is in big trouble. He has defeated and killed the prophets of Baal, but then the evil queen, Jezebel, promises to have him killed by the next day. This throws Elijah into a major depression, and he has had enough and wishes he could die. An angel comes and encourages him to eat, and he then travels 40 days and 40 nights to Mount Horeb.

There, on the mountain, God shows Elijah something important. God says that he will pass by. Then a wind comes up, so strong that it can tear mountains apart. But Elijah does not sense God in the wind. There follows an earthquake, and finally a fire, but God is not in either. Then comes a gentle whisper. God does not speak to Elijah in the wind, the earthquake or the fire, but in a whisper.

And so it can be for us. God frequently speaks to us not by spectacular signs, but in a whisper. He is often there in the quiet as the still, small voice of calm. How can we learn to listen for the voice and for the whisper?

PRAYER
Lord God,
I pray that you will speak clearly to me today,
whether in the wind, earthquake or fire,
or in a quiet whisper.
Amen

6

Christian reflections on environmental issues

These reflections are written as a companion to *A Christian Guide to Environmental Issues*, second edition (BRF, 2021). The book explores eight key environmental issues:

1. **Biodiversity** loss is now at a critical level, with a massive decline in biodiversity over the past 50 years. It is not just the loss of individual species or organisms but whole habitats are disappearing.
2. The crisis of **climate change** is much in the news, and severe weather events are being reported from many parts of the world. We explore what has led us into this crisis and how we should respond as Christians.
3. In a world with a changing climate, **water** is a major issue. Over two billion people in the world still do not have access to fresh water, and our misuse of water has negative impacts on the natural world.
4. People often raise high **human population** as a big environmental issue. It is an important factor to consider, but when you look at environmental destruction this is more often driven by the **consumption** of countries with low birth rates. These two issues need to be considered together.

5 **Energy** and how we power our society, has always been an important issue, and over the generations we have progressed in our use of different types of energy. We are now starting to make the first big shift in many generations to leaving fossil fuels behind and returning to renewable sources of energy, using technology to aid efficiency.

6 **Soil** is an often-neglected subject, and yet we depend on it for life. This thin and complex material has chemical and biological cycles within it which determine whether it continues to support life.

7 Soil supports **food**, and how we grow our food has a big impact on the ecology of the world.

8 Finally, **environment and sustainable development** interact, and we need to look towards sustainability in all parts of the world as we seek especially to support the poorest people who suffer most from environmental problems.

We explore each of these themes in *A Christian Guide to Environmental Issues* and reflect on them from a Christian perspective. These reflections follow the same themes from a spiritual perspective, helping us to use them to better connect with God, people and nature. Following the book chapters, we begin with a reflection on 'Love' to introduce the series and we end with one on 'Hope' to collect our thoughts together and see how God can guide us hopefully through the environmental crisis as we trust in him.

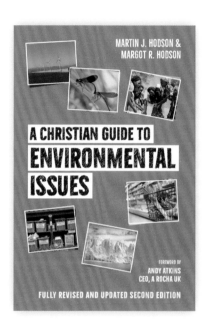

Environmental sustainability is a major issue for us all. In this extensively updated edition, Martin and Margot Hodson consider eight key environmental issues: **biodiversity, climate change, water, population and consumption, energy, soil, food, and environment and sustainable development**.

Through ethical reflections, Bible studies on a different biblical doctrine for each chapter, and eco-tips to enable a practical response, they outline the biblical basis for care of the environment and help the reader integrate environmental thinking and Christian faith.

A Christian Guide to Environmental Issues

Martin J. Hodson and Margot R. Hodson

978 1 80039 005 8 £9.99

brfonline.org.uk

1 Love is the key

Luke 10:25–28

An expert in the law stood up to test Jesus. 'Teacher,' he asked, 'what must I do to inherit eternal life?' 'What is written in the Law?' he replied. 'How do you read it?' He answered, '"Love the Lord your God with all your heart and with all your soul and with all your strength and with all your mind"; and, "Love your neighbour as yourself."' 'You have answered correctly,' Jesus replied. 'Do this and you will live.'

If you were given a Post-it note and asked to write down the message of the Bible, what would you write? In Jesus' day, asking for summaries of the law was common. With the whole of the biblical text to work through, what was the most important message?

A popular method was to combine two texts that had a common word, to reveal an important truth. Jesus took the common word 'love' to show that love is at the heart of our faith. We should love God, our neighbour and ourselves.

When he was asked, 'Who is my neighbour?', Jesus responded with the story of the good Samaritan. This is so familiar to us that we easily forget how shocking it was in Jesus' day, when Samaritans were looked down upon. Jesus challenged his hearers to have a broader view of who might be a neighbour and who might show love.

How might Jesus challenge us? Who might we not see as neighbours and how might we widen those we love as ourselves? These studies are an opportunity to explore our responsibility to all of God's creation. Caring for God's world shows our love for him and ourselves.

PRAYER
Dear Lord, help us to love you more through the love we show to others, including other creatures. Help us to respect your creation as love-filled and love-giving. Amen

2 A sabbath rest for all creatures

Exodus 20:8–11

Remember the Sabbath day by keeping it holy. Six days you shall labour and do all your work, but the seventh day is a sabbath to the Lord your God. On it you shall not do any work, neither you, nor your son or daughter, nor your male or female servant, nor your animals, nor any foreigner residing in your towns. For in six days the Lord made the heavens and the earth, the sea, and all that is in them, but he rested on the seventh day. Therefore the Lord blessed the Sabbath day and made it holy.

I (Margot) can remember learning the ten commandments at school. They were one of the few things that we learned by heart and they felt very important. I wonder how many children have learned these commandments over the thousands of years of their history? Their endurance indicates their strength in setting out how we should live in relation to God, other people and the rest of God's creation.

When I learned them all those years ago, I was especially impressed that the commandment about the sabbath mentioned giving rest to your animals. On this holy day, every creature should rest and have time to recharge.

In the 2020 lockdown at the start of the Covid-19 pandemic, we saw the benefit to nature when human activity paused. Animals were more visible in urban areas and birdsong became a message of hope. With very little traffic, fewer hedgehogs died crossing roads and birds bred more successfully in areas normally filled with tourists.

In normal times, the lack of rest is having a terrible impact on our world's biodiversity. In the long term this threatens not only the wild species of our planet, but also our own existence. In addition, many domestic animals around the world are kept in poor conditions on factory farms. How might we make space for nature to have its sabbaths every year and not just during a pandemic?

PRAYER

Lord, give us courage to keep your sabbath and show how to better provide sabbath for all creatures that dwell on Earth. Amen

3 Broken covenant, damaged climate

Isaiah 24:4–5

The earth dries up and withers, the world languishes and withers,
the heavens languish with the earth. The earth is defiled by its people;
they have disobeyed the laws, violated the statutes and broken the
everlasting covenant.

Drought is a terrible thing. It leads to famine, and famine leads to hunger, desperation and death. Isaiah describes his experience of drought and links it to human activity. In our own society, we now know that the burning of fossil fuel is leading to a warming of our global climate, which is causing negative impacts across the world. One of the most unjust impacts is that those who have contributed least to the problem are suffering the most from the consequences, especially from droughts and floods.

Isaiah declares that the people have broken God's everlasting covenant. The Hebrew scriptures set out just relationships between people, God and the land. When these relationships are abused, the covenant is broken and there are negative consequences.

This is a bleak message, but there is hope. The second part of Isaiah sets out the joy that God has in restoring those relationships when the people have returned to live in the covenant relationship they were always intended to have. Isaiah 35 describes the desert bursting into flower and water pouring forth.

How can we each play our part to restore the broken covenant and establish just relationships with the earth and other people? Think of one practical thing that you could do this week.

PRAYER
Lord, give us wisdom to know how to live simply and justly in this age of climate crisis. Amen

4 Water of life

Isaiah 55:10–11

As the rain and the snow come down from heaven, and do not return to it without watering the earth and making it bud and flourish, so that it yields seed for the sower and bread for the eater, so is my word that goes out from my mouth: it will not return to me empty, but will accomplish what I desire and achieve the purpose for which I sent it.

For some years we taught a course on Bible and environment for a summer school based in a fairy-tale castle in the Austrian Alps. We loved teaching young adults from many countries, and we enjoyed the stunningly beautiful scenery. As we walked up through the mountains, we would see waterfalls and snow on the peaks. The alpine pastures were vibrant with wildflowers and the sound of cow bells. It seemed the most beautiful place on earth.

Isaiah uses the image of a fruitful landscape to teach us about faith. Rain is essential for all of life. The rich alpine pastures thrive on the mountain rains and snowmelt and crops are dependent on them.

Jesus is the Living Word and the Bread of Life. When we receive him, we receive all that we need in life and death. We use the fruit of the earth for the bread and wine of communion. As we take these gifts, we are given a foretaste of the restored creation, where we will one day live together in peace. In the beauty of the earth and in the mystery of communion, we glimpse salvation for ourselves and for the whole of God's creation.

PRAYER
Lord, when we see the beauty of your creation,
fix our eyes on your purposes. Help us to be
strengthened through the vision of restored creation,
to serve you now and bring joy and hope to those
around us. Amen

5 Making choices in our crowded consumer world

1 Peter 4:10–11 (abridged)

Each of you should use whatever gift you have received to serve others, as faithful stewards of God's grace in its various forms… so that in all things God may be praised through Jesus Christ.

When lockdown happened in spring 2020, shopping became more and less complicated: more complicated because of all the restrictions, and less complicated because we all simply made do. We used up flour and other dried and tinned items in the cupboards that had been hanging around for a long time. We didn't think of buying clothes, because a change of a pair of jeans, a few T-shirts and a couple of 'Zoom shirts' seemed to do the trick. Though we weren't major buyers of fashion or other items, we had been consumers. It was good to stop and reflect.

In rebuilding our world, we need to prioritise ways of living lightly, to give the planet space to renew itself. This means finding ways to build an economy that is not based around endless consumerism and waste. Our world is highly interconnected but continues injustices from the past, with millions of people living in poverty. How can we rebuild a fairer global economy that will eradicate poverty and help to stabilise human population without increasing consumerism?

We have had a harsh light shone on many aspects of our world that are unjust and unsustainable. Our task is to use our gifts to be part of building a better world and one that points more clearly towards God's peaceable kingdom.

PRAYER
Lord, help us, in rebuilding our world, to build one that points towards your kingdom of peace and justice for all people and creation. Amen

6 Energy: needing to do things differently

Matthew 9:16–17

No one sews a patch of unshrunk cloth on an old garment, for the patch will pull away from the garment, making the tear worse. Neither do people pour new wine into old wineskins. If they do, the skins will burst; the wine will run out, and the wineskins will be ruined. No, they pour new wine into new wineskins, and both are preserved.

My favourite pair of jeans finally wore a hole, and I (Margot) needed to buy a new pair. I had to shorten them and thought the piece I had cut off the bottom of my new pair might be perfect to patch my much-loved old pair. But when I pinned the patch to sew it, I remembered this parable – it was too new and would have torn the old fabric, worn thin through wearing. Instead I found an older piece of fabric to make the patch.

Our 1940s vicarage needs adapting to make it suitable for a post-carbon future. This will not be easy, but it has already been adapted once, from fireplaces to oil-fired central heating. It can be done again, but it will need creative thinking.

We need to live our lives differently to avoid environmental catastrophe. This is not easy, as we have lived our lives in a world dependant on fossil fuels. We need to pause, take stock of our lives and see what we might do differently. We may find that the new direction is more life-giving than the old.

PRAYER
Lord, help us to have the courage to stop, reflect and pray. Show us the new ways that we can live in harmony with your creation. Amen

7 Exploring the soil of our lives

Matthew 13:8

Still other seed fell on good soil, where it produced a crop – a hundred, sixty or thirty times what was sown.

Jesus understood soil, and he challenged our faith through different outcomes for seed depending on where it fell. Falling on the path points to a lack of understanding, rocky ground indicates faith with shallow roots, weeds are the troubles of this world and good soil is when faith grows and is fruitful.

We all like to think that we are the good soil; we have received faith joyfully, and we are, we hope, producing a good crop. But what if it is not that simple? Suppose we are all a bit of each of these categories? There are some things that always leave us with questions, and we are confused like the seed on the path. Sometimes we are like rocky ground, and our spiritual roots can feel shallow. Maybe that is you at the moment and God is feeling distant. Then who of us does not have some troubles in this life? These can feel like weeds choking us. When we come to God, we have assurance that we are truly rooted in the good soil and are close to him.

For many of us, we will show some aspects of all four hearers and all four types of soil. For some of us we will cycle through phases in our life where we are closer to God or further apart. If we are honest, none of us is ever totally in the good soil. What can we do to move more of our roots into the good soil?

PRAYER

Dear Lord, help us to nurture the good soil in our lives and to trust you when we find ourselves on more difficult ground. Give us roots to our faith that will keep us close to you in all that life brings us. Amen

8 Food for life

John 6:35

Then Jesus declared, 'I am the bread of life. Whoever comes to me will never go hungry, and whoever believes in me will never be thirsty.'

When we moved to our new vicarage in west Oxfordshire, we swapped a suburban garden for a rambling country garden with an enormous veg patch that was more like a field. A previous family had kept pigs, and we were keen to capitalise on the enriched soil to see what we could grow. We soon had several plots with lots of seedlings busting up as the sun shone through in the spring.

For all our care and watering, we made several mistakes. We failed to spot potato blight and had to do an emergency dig to rescue our spuds before they succumbed, and our beans were too much in the shade and stayed small and weedy. But we did have a stunning patch of parsley, amazing parsnips and wonderful Brussel sprouts. We will be just a little more experienced next year, but we are also thankful that we don't depend on the food we have grown to live. If we did, we would go hungry.

Millions of people in our world face hunger through climate change, soil degradation, poverty and the impact of the Covid-19 pandemic. John records that Jesus fed the hungry crowds and afterwards declared that he is the Bread of Life. As Christians we can follow Christ by bringing both practical and spiritual support to others. Let us be sustained by Jesus the Bread of Life, as we enable others to have bread to meet their hunger and receive life.

PRAYER

Dear Lord, as we see so many people go hungry in our world, give us compassion, give us the means of enabling change and give us hope to bring to others. Amen

9 Environment and global justice

2 Corinthians 5:18

All this is from God, who reconciled us to himself through Christ and gave us the ministry of reconciliation.

Summer 2020 will be remembered for the pandemic and the Black Lives Matter demonstrations. The events of that year exposed racial inequality in multiple ways. As demonstrations rippled around the world, so the depth of inequality became shockingly exposed: centuries of exploitation has left many nations in the global South depleted of wealth and infrastructure; centuries of exploitation and discrimination have left many from black and ethnic minority backgrounds in richer countries at a socio-economic disadvantage. Human poverty and environmental degradation go hand in hand. They need to be tackled together by nations and agencies working in collaboration.

How can Christians play our part in bringing reconciliation to the world? Paul shared with the Christians in Corinth that God had given them the 'ministry of reconciliation'. This was an important task, but it was not one that they would have to tackle alone. It is a ministry that God has given us, and he will equip us for this purpose.

Take a look at the context in which you live and your own personal circumstances. How might you take a further step in your reconciliation ministry as Christ's ambassador? It may be something very small that seems insignificant, or it may be something bigger that you are nervous of stepping into. Pray about your thoughts, share with others who know you well and take a step forward as you are guided.

PRAYER

Lord, thank you for reconciling us through Christ so we can know your love and come before you. We feel humbled and inadequate when we hear your call to take up our ministry of reconciliation. Help us to trust in you as we step forward to take our place in bringing healing to your world. Amen

10 A covenant for hope

Hebrews 6:19

We have this hope as an anchor for the soul, firm and secure.

A few years ago, I (Margot) was asked to lead collective worship for younger children at our church school on the theme of hope. It was the school's value for the term and they wanted something memorable for the children. I took this Bible verse but explained it more simply as 'God's hope is an anchor that keeps us safe and steady'. Ever since I have valued this paraphrase and often think of it when life gets tough.

We completed writing these studies at the end of 2020. I had spoken on God's anchor of hope at one of our last church visits in February of that year, and it continued to resource me as the months unfolded. We looked back on that eventful year with terrific sadness for the pain and bereavement that so many had suffered and were still suffering around the world.

We cannot predict what the future will hold. We know we face severe challenges with climate change, human health, economic crisis and huge injustice. We pray that world leaders will find a way forward to deal with all these issues together. But whatever happens, we continue to hold on to our covenant hope in Christ as we seek to play our small part in building a just and sustainable world. We are strengthened by words from Hebrews 6:19 and may you also find the anchor of hope in Christ and may God lead you onward in faith.

PRAYER
Lord, lead us forward in practical ways to care for people and your precious creation. Give us hope in our hearts and strength to serve you in these challenging times. Amen

Closing thoughts

This century is going to be tough. Climate change is already having major impacts around the world, which are going to become even more severe as the planet heats up. Combine this with the other problems we have outlined, and we face a difficult future. In our response, we need to think through the actions that could point to hope. As a church, we are in a unique position. Our international network of grass-roots communities gives us insights into conditions in other parts of the world. We must keep these insights strong, to maintain support for some of the poorest in the world; there will be some in society who will want to pull up the drawbridge.

Locally we will also find ourselves in communities that are increasingly under pressure. As we recover from the Covid-19 pandemic and climate change brings about further disruptive weather events, how will we move forward? How will we cope with very different circumstances in future? We have the spiritual resources to enable others to adjust to these difficulties, but we need to engage with our local communities to be able to use them. We have an amazing Christian hope. As we face a world in difficulty, each one of us is invited to respond to the challenge of making that hope visible to others. A few questions to leave you with:

- Our studies have shown that we hope for a renewed creation. Some people suggest that this means Christians need not worry about environmental care now. How would you respond to this argument?

- Climate change and environmental refugees are already a real phenomenon. How will we speak up for these people and make sure that room is made for them in the rest of the world, including our own land?

- What do we need to do now to prepare our churches to be willing and able to support the poorer parts of the world, as things continue to get tougher towards the middle of the century?

- How can we best be examples of Christian hope to the people around us? What does this say about the way we might approach mission this century?

As we have progressed through *Green Reflections*, we have seen how the Bible is full of teaching about nature and how that relates to the rest of life. The reflections have not just applied to our relationship with the natural world but have seen how lessons from the natural world apply to all aspects of our lives. Our responsibility to care for God's creation is an integral part of our faith and it interacts with the whole of our life and our relationship with God. Our reflections have mirrored the breadth of an inclusive view of the world, where faith matters in every aspect of our lives. We hope that as you close this book, you will be inspired to reflect this integration in your life and faith.

Further reading

Richard Bauckham, *Bible and Ecology: Rediscovering the community of creation* (DLT, 2010).

Dave Bookless, *Planetwise: Dare to care for God's world* (IVP, 2008).

Martin J. Hodson and Margot R. Hodson, *A Christian Guide to Environmental Issues*, second edition (BRF, 2021).

Mark Maslin, *Climate Change: A very short introduction*, third edition (Oxford University Press, 2014).

Ruth Valerio, *Saying Yes to Life* (SPCK, 2019).

Ruth Valerio, Martin J. Hodson, Margot R. Hodson and Timothy Howles, *Covid-19: Environment, justice, and the future* (Grove, 2020).

Useful websites

A Rocha, Christians in Conservation, is an international organisation with centres in many countries. **arocha.org**

Christian Rural and Environmental Studies (CRES) runs certificate and diploma courses by distance learning. CRES is run jointly by the John Ray Initiative and A Rocha UK, and is validated by Ripon College, Cuddesdon, near Oxford. **cres.org.uk**

Eco Church is an ecumenical programme in England and Wales helping churches to make the link between environmental issues and Christian faith. The programme is administered by A Rocha UK. **ecochurch.arocha.org.uk**

The John Ray Initiative (JRI) aims to bring together Christian and scientific understanding of the environment. **jri.org.uk**

Acknowledgements

Unless otherwise stated, scripture quotations are taken from The Holy Bible, New International Version (Anglicised edition) copyright © 1979, 1984, 2011 by Biblica. Used by permission of Hodder & Stoughton Publishers, a Hachette UK company. All rights reserved. 'NIV' is a registered trademark of Biblica. UK trademark number 1448790.

Scripture quotations marked NRSV are taken from The New Revised Standard Version of the Bible, Anglicised edition, copyright © 1989, 1995 by the Division of Christian Education of the National Council of the Churches of Christ in the United States of America. Used by permission. All rights reserved.

Scripture quotations marked KJV are taken from the Authorised Version of the Bible (The King James Bible), the rights in which are vested in the Crown, are reproduced by permission of the Crown's Patentee, Cambridge University Press.

Every effort has been made to trace and contact copyright owners for material used in this resource. We apologise for any inadvertent omissions or errors, and would ask those concerned to contact us so that full acknowledgement can be made in the future.

About the artist

Born in London in 1958, **Martin Beek** has been drawing and painting since he was a young boy. He studied Fine Art at Exeter University and has exhibited widely throughout his life. His earlier paintings consist mainly of landscapes in oil and pastel of America, where he has travelled extensively and directed the arts programme at a children's summer camp. In more recent years he has held residencies at Wellington College and Marlborough College in the UK and focused on *plein air* landscapes in Oxfordshire and Berkshire. He is currently giving online art history talks for Ardington School of Crafts. He is a member of St Luke's Church, Oxford.

Index of Bible references

Readings in standard typeface are the main ones used for the reflections. Those in *italics* are cited in the reflection texts.

Subject index

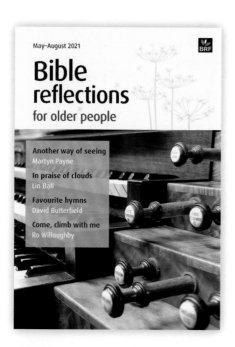

May–August 2021

BRF

Bible reflections

for older people

Another way of seeing
Martyn Payne

In praise of clouds
Lin Ball

Favourite hymns
David Butterfield

Come, climb with me
Ro Willoughby

A daily companion to keep by your side

Written by older people for older people, these reflections are designed to bring hope, assurance and sustenance, reminding the reader of the presence and love of God. Each issue contains 40 Bible reflections and prayer suggestions to use and revisit as often as is needed.

In the central section, Pioneer of BRF's Anna Chaplaincy for Older People ministry **Debbie Thrower** offers interviews and ideas to encourage and inspire.

Edited by Eley McAinsh
Single copy £5.25
brfonline.org.uk

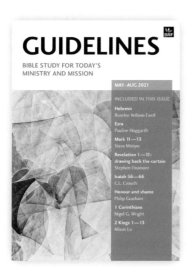

GUIDELINES

BIBLE STUDY FOR TODAY'S MINISTRY AND MISSION

MAY–AUG 2021

INCLUDED IN THIS ISSUE

Hebrews
Roselee Velloso Ewell

Ezra
Pauline Hoggarth

Mark 11—13
Steve Motyer

Revelation 1—11: drawing back the curtain
Stephen Finamore

Isaiah 56—66
C.L. Crouch

Honour and shame
Philip Grasham

1 Corinthians
Nigel G. Wright

2 Kings 1—13
Alison Lo

Edited by Helen Paynter
Single copy £4.75
brfonline.org.uk

Guidelines is a unique Bible reading resource that offers four months of in-depth study, drawing on the insights of current scholarship. Its intention is to enable all its readers to interpret and apply the biblical text with confidence in today's world, while helping to equip church leaders as they meet the challenges of mission and disciple-building.

Instead of the usual dated daily readings, it provides weekly units, broken into six sections, plus an introduction giving context for the passage, and a final section of points for thought and prayer. On any day you can read as many or as few sections as you wish.

Also available as an app for Android, iPhone and iPad.

Enabling all ages to grow in faith

Anna Chaplaincy
Living Faith
Messy Church
Parenting for Faith

The Bible Reading Fellowship (BRF) is a Christian charity that resources individuals and churches. Our vision is to enable people of all ages to grow in faith and understanding of the Bible and to see more people equipped to exercise their gifts in leadership and ministry.

To find out more about our work, visit
brf.org.uk